A CO

PERSI ___ ___

A CONVICT'S PERSPECTIVE

Critiquing Penology and Inmate Rehabilitation

T. LAMONT BAKER

Foreword by: J. Vincent Hurley

Printed in the United States

ISBN-13:978-1491242322

Additional copies of this book can be ordered at
www.amazon.com

"…Write about this young man squeezing drop by drop the [convict] out of himself and waking one fine morning feeling that real human blood, not a [convict's], is flowing in his veins."
— Anton Chekhov

"To be modern is to have the courage to use one's critical intelligence to question and challenge the prevailing authorities, powers and hierarchies of the world."
— Cornel West

"But in general I feel better, and no less radical, and you will feel better too, I guarantee, once you leave hold of the doctrinaire, and allow your chain-less mind to do its own thinking."
— Christopher Hitchens

"Prison life destroys thought utterly."
— Antonio Gramsci

Table of Contents

FOREWORD

I met Baker in the fall of 2008. I was housed in dorm 2B, on Unit Four, at Pasquotank Correctional Institution for a couple of months before Baker arrived. When he walked into the dorm, I must admit that I immediately labeled him as "just another young dummy." He had extremely wild, unkempt dreadlocks and a very serious demeanor. He kind of reminded me of an angry black Sideshow Bob (from *The Simpsons*).

I won't bore you with details here– this isn't a sappy memoir. Let's just say that Baker and I eventually befriended each other. We had many interests in common, similar senses of humor, lengthy sentences, and a mutual hatred of prison. Most importantly, we each knew we were more intellectually advanced than the "average" inmate; we each knew we were *Incarcerated Thinkers*.

Incarcerated Thinkers is a term used to refer to inmates who are passionate about what Dr. Cornel West once referred to as the Life of the Mind. These convicts are in the highest percentiles, as far as intelligence goes. They are well informed in fields such as politics, entrepreneurship, convict criminology, black history, feminism, and religion. Their status as Incarcerated Thinkers is well deserved. Some of them have specific academic concentrations, and some simply have a very broad, yet impressive, academic scope. A few of them are products of academia, while others are thoroughly self-educated. Regardless of which category these prisoners fall in, one thing is for certain– Incarcerated Thinkers are all intellectual TITANS!

Baker is one of the most dynamic members of this elite class of prisoners, as the pages that follow will demonstrate. He first expressed his intention to write such pages while we were housed at Johnston

Correctional Institution in Smithfield, North Carolina. He told me that he wanted to write a book that spreads awareness of our experiences as Incarcerated Thinkers and generates a debate over the stances that we've taken regarding certain penal mechanisms. He also told me this was the first step towards widespread change— towards shifting prison's raison d'etre from crime promotion to rehabilitation.

Upon hearing my intellectual cohort's thoughts, I decided to play devil's advocate. Specifically, I told him that rehabilitation simply can't be the core of North Carolina's penal system; at the very best, it could only serve as prison's theoretical, if not rhetorical, framework. In less flowery language this pretty much means that most prisoners have never been habilitated, therefore *RE*habilitating them wasn't possible.

Baker agreed with this part of my argument, as I knew he would. (He frequently uses the word "habilitation" throughout this book.) The second part of my argument, however, didn't go as smoothly. As a matter of fact, Baker didn't even consider my position once I made it clear to him. Now, I'm so very glad that he didn't.

The second part of my argument was presented in typical Incarcerated Thinker fashion. There was a lot of profanity, an array of jokes, some nasty insults, a bunch of laughter, and a few *Family Guy* references, but I'll clean it up slightly for the sake of decency. Basically, I told Baker that just because he possesses the ability to explain our plights doesn't mean that he would do so in a way that would ultimately penetrate the apathetic borders of his readers' consciences. I made it clear to him that his provocative and sometimes radical style of expression was effective amongst Incarcerated Thinkers, but it probably wouldn't be sharp enough to pierce the altruistic cores of his readers' hearts. Truthfully speaking, I was of the opinion that prison reform advocates had discussed many of the same topics he would address in his writings. Because those colloquies failed to produce substantial penological improvements, I surmised that Baker's book would also reach an identical end.

Debating prison's flaws and mass incarceration in general, like many other hot button topics prevalent in our society, tends to travel along a trajectory akin to a religious revival's advent into a foreign land. Initially, the missionaries' presence is welcomed with vast amounts of intrigue, enthusiasm, and promise by the locals. Unfortunately, soon after the missionaries' departure, the once open-minded euphoria gradually reverts back to the lull of the status quo and nothing of significance gets accomplished in the visited territory.

Unless Baker could manage to provide profound, lasting alternatives to penology's common rhetoric, he would appear redundant and only contribute to what has become essentially "white noise" concerning effective inmate habilitation. I believed it was more beneficial for him to focus on self-improvement measures (i.e. acquiring vocational trades, avid reading, and vicarious correspondence courses) while in prison rather than pursuing a futile cause that would surely conclude with his disappointment. I soon learned how incorrect my assessments were. It only took a couple of our informal think-tank sessions for Baker to help me appreciate how his book would meet the criteria necessary to become a sublime tool instrumental in the construction of a better society. Baker dispelled my initial trepidations by revealing the uniqueness of his book's perspective, the far reaching magnitude of its objectives, and how it supersedes any current resource available to the Incarcerated Thinkers as it pertains to their continual pursuit of intellectual development.

At this point, I'm both thankful and sad as I anticipate this book's publication. I'm thankful because the Universe granted me the opportunity to be a part of this evolutionary work (which will soon grow beyond its current status of success d'estime). I'm also sad because I'm witnessing the countless obstacles my dear comrade is enduring just to share with the public his vision of obtaining optimal habilitation. As mentioned in his book's preface, from a lack of the most basic tools (computer access, updated resources, pencils, erasers, etc.) to the presence of staunch opposition (harassment, administrative threats of confiscation, disciplinary actions, etc.), it should be considered a quasi-miracle that Baker's book is currently available for rendering. The very fact that you are reading this work may inadvertently numb you to the reality of our unrelenting struggle for psychogenetic development. Be assured though, with each passing day, the gulf between adequate and inadequate habilitation deepens, swallowing up many potential contributors to our society.

    A Convict's Perspective addresses this injustice and emphasizes the need for implementing revolutionary-style habilitative practices throughout North Carolina's penal institutions. It theorizes that the most effective way for incarcerated individuals to achieve elite level habilitation and transcend their criminal lots is to have the opportunity to obtain knowledge and training equivalent to that of the most productive members of our society. In this book, Baker provides a comprehensive look into the misguided direction of prison's educative and rehabilitative initiatives, the unfortunate consequences of such initiatives, and who shoulders a large responsibility in reshaping the façade of penal reform. His writings accurately illustrate the distended intellectual stomachs of a scholastically starved sub-group and the malnourished minds of an academically anorexic minority. This pitiable population is desperately craving a seat at society's table of opportunities, but so far they've been doomed to nibble on the repugnant carrion of prison's valueless programs.

    Baker presents this message without focusing solely on the scarred emotional psyche of inmates. He complements such a focus by pointing out how this denial of opportunity is a key component to the return feast that over seventy percent of North Carolina's captives re-eat again and again at prisons' diner of intellectual destitute. He also candidly exposes the fraud being perpetrated throughout the North Carolina Department of Public Safety/Division of Adult Correction— Prisons' dilapidated educational programs. This deception, this skullduggery, only adds to the false narrative found in this state— one of hopelessly unmotivated convicts choosing to reject "quality" educational opportunities and instead deciding to relapse into criminal behavior and re-enter prison's revolving doors. This skewed view only compounds the stigma society places on all inmates and increases the divide between civilization and detention centers' denizens. This, in essence, undermines any attempt to invoke richly fertile habilitation, and it is to the detriment of everyone involved.

A Convict's Perspective avoids the dangers associated with assuming the role of the victim by legitimizing its message with tangible solutions and a proactive approach to prison reform. The brilliant manner, in which this book strategically directs its pleas of assistance towards members of academia, namely penology and its subsets, increases the likelihood that affluent ideas and progressive agendas will emerge from those with the most significant influence in these critical areas. It challenges the intelligentsia to gaze introspectively. It makes academics question whether they will continue to adhere to the current comatose curriculum of criminology or instead begin to belligerently mangle the malignant mole that adorns the face of their academic arenas, the dark cloud looming over their chosen scholastic fields. Complacency and inactivity have become norms concerning North Carolina's recidivism epidemic, and A Convict's Perspective is Baker's official call to action. From enriching academia and private enterprise, to increasing public confidence through inmates' intellectual and psychological restoration, Baker shows how mutually beneficial it would be for our state's leaders to look into adopting his thought-provoking principles.

Incarcerated Thinkers have fought valiantly in combating penal oppression. Baker has championed the righteous cause of giving a voice to society's silenced, to North Carolina's prodigal children seeking acceptance from our countrymen and pursuing the comfort of this state's habilitative embrace. For his efforts, he should be encouraged and commended.

Webster's New Pocket Dictionary simply but eloquently defines a patriot as "one who loves and defends his or her country." Baker embodies the true principles behind that title with his bold, progressive actions. Contemporary reformists have an unconventional yet monumental ally in their uphill battle for social change. I just hope they will use him effectively. I'm confident that after thoroughly examining *A Convict's Perspective*, you will draw a conclusion similar to the one I hold concerning Baker's potential: no longer wondering about "*what could have been*" to now optimistic regarding "*what is to come.*"

— J. Vincent Hurley
Inmate# 1097591

13

PREFACE

The following text is a product of much intellectual labor— hard, strenuous, and very exhausting mental labor, to be exact. This labor, this "mind-breaking" work, began long before I made the decision to document my experiential observations in the form of a book. When I think back to the beginning of this intellectual labor I'm reminded of the latter parts of my teenage years which were spent in a jail in Durham, North Carolina. It was during this period of my life that I went from being an aspiring college student to being an inmate in a cell, pondering on some of the things that would eventually become the content presented here in *A Convict's Perspective*. This frightened teenager, deficient in worldly wisdom, had no idea that he would eventually grow to become the man that is writing these words. He didn't know that he would one day develop a sincere desire to feed influential academics with his ripening intellectual fruit.

This lost and misguided teenager had only one concern regarding his future; he had only one dominating interest regarding what he believed was upcoming inevitabilities. This concern, this consumptive interest, was his release from detention. He honestly believed that he would walk out of the Durham County Jail as a free man. Although he was privy to egregious instances of injustice for which the legal system was often responsible, he still had faith in those that were charged with applying and enforcing North Carolina's laws.

This mature child was somewhat aware of the criminal justice system's history of mistreating young, ebony-skinned male defendants, but he didn't think that HE would ever be mangled by rabid court officials and snarling agents of mass imprisonment. (He didn't know that he could get a life sentence for murder even though someone else had already confessed to and been convicted of the killing and all involved parties knew, and stated in court, that he had murdered no one.) He didn't view himself as a serious delinquent, and he thought that once other people saw what he saw in himself, he would avoid being digested by the Jim Crow-like criminal designation. He believed that if other people came to realize that he wasn't a societal miscreant, he wouldn't be torn and shredded by the mouth of the penal establishment which has police officers for incisors, attorneys and judges for canines, and prison officials for bicuspids and molars.

     I shake my head and chuckle now as I look back at my naiveté. I can't help but wonder how the teenage "me" — precocious, yet marked by unaffected simplicity— would have fared had I been released and had my paradigm been congruent to and in accord with reality. I can only imagine the heights I would've reached had I not been relegated to almost a lifetime in prison — a human kennel where talent is wasted, minds and morals deteriorate, and "black-male-as-predator" stereotypes are promoted and endorsed.

     In 2009, about three years into the personal and unorthodox maturation process that I experienced as a teenager— a process that resulted in what is now a critical and philanthropic intellectual freedom fighter— the first of many impetuses for *A Convict's Perspective* occurred here in the state of North Carolina. Then governor Beverly Purdue refused to permit a significant number of inmates to be released from confinement even though their sentences had been served. Mrs. Purdue believed these prisoners should remain incarcerated because she *FELT* that at the time they were sentenced (in the 1970's), the sentencing laws were too lenient.

     I did what most convicts did upon receiving this information: I imagined myself in their situation. I imagined spending thirty-five or forty years in prison, anticipating my eventual release every day, only to be told that the governor has now made it so that my "eventual release" will never come. I pictured years being wasted proving that I'm no longer a danger to local communities, and then I thought of myself being informed that instead of being released from prison after multiple decades, I would now die incarcerated. (In case you didn't know, after dying in prison my family would have to buy my body from the state if they wanted to give me a decent funeral; but after being absent for almost four decades I wouldn't expect this financial transaction to happen.) This will occur not because I've committed new crimes or accumulated new charges, not because I'm mentally unstable, not because I'm a threat to society's sense of security, and not because my exodus from imprisonment will change anyone's life other than my own. This will occur solely because of someone's emotions.

Regardless of what the laws stated at the time of my detention, I must now die behind bars to make a complete stranger feel better. Who knew that conforming to the ideals of judicial and executive elites and molding oneself to fit into their particular perceptions of acceptability mattered more than the fulfillment of what the law defined as justice? The world's "moral monarch," a state in the Bible Belt, legislators that allegedly exemplify Christian principles such as forgiveness and compassion, are spending time, a decade into the new millennium, ensuring that my actions forty years ago (when most of these congressmen were in grade school) block my release from the state's social trash can. Imagining myself in such a situation, (a situation that is a reality for many of my older fellow inmates) aroused such acute anger and frustration within me that it almost became overwhelming. In order to get my anger to dissipate I had to remind myself that this wasn't my reality.

After this dissipation, I began to question how frequently the opposite scenario occurred. I wondered if municipal executives and bureaucrats in this state had ever so passionately rallied for the release of inmates

16

who they believed should be exonerated for whatever reason. After extensive research, mainly in the form of interviews, questionnaires, and second-hand internet searches, I reached appalling conclusions. I could not find one example of an executive action that was taken by this state to prevent further incarceration of someone that didn't deserve it. Although many inmates have been released after it was determined that they were wrongfully convicted, I couldn't locate a single instance where the North Carolina government so adamantly opposed the continued imprisonment of a group of convicts. In other words, here in this state, the idea of opposing someone's imprisonment has never led to changes in criminal law, penal practices, nor sentencing guidelines. This notion also has never led a state executive to actively pursue the prevention of future episodes of unwanted and unwarranted incarceration.

I found this imbalance, this invocation of such lopsided legislation, to be both troubling and intriguing. For lawmakers and agents of law enforcement to initiate and promote such a nonsymmetrical execution of responsibilities was suspiciously conniving and fretfully fascinating. At least that's how I felt at the time. Looking back, I can't help but view this old "feeling" of mine as a very good thing. Better yet, it was a *great* thing because this "feeling" eventually became my motivation. Being confronted with such a perplexing reality, my body and my intellect inexplicably developed a deep desire to pay closer attention, to gather more information, to compose my findings and interpret my thoughts in a manner that both illuminated and inspired. Thus began my quest to examine and criticize this state's historically onerous and dispirited penal system, a system that has repeatedly made a spectacle of contributing to the destruction of young— predominantly black— male lives.

This quest of mine has uncovered a plethora of harsh realities. This journey has unearthed both North Carolina prisons' tendency to do nothing other than deepen criminous sentiments as well as the administration's inflexible opposition to doing something meaningful to correct such deepening. It has shed light upon the demonization and punishment of detention residents simply for being uneducated, and the wicked systemic efforts to deny these residents access to the latest emerging movement in higher education— open educational resources and massive open online courses.

My quest has taken me across many lands. I've been through treacherous jungles of abuse dispensed by malevolent correctional officers. I've traversed barren sun-baked deserts of deprivation of opportunity and denial of hope, and explored deep oceans of iniquity filled with incarcerated whales, exhausted from swimming three times as hard, yet making only a third of the progress of their "less restricted" aquatic counterparts. Each stop along my journey thus far has been documented here in *A Convict's Perspective*.

I've avoided hyperbole at all costs, mainly because its usage isn't necessary to transmit my opinions, theories and ideas. This work is also void of literary pageantry, poetic story-telling, and excessively artful and ostentatious linguistic forms, for my goal was never to amuse nor entertain those who read simply for pleasure. Quite the contrary, my goal is, and always has been, to complement and enlighten scholars and to provoke activists into engagement. My unwavering aim is, and will continue to be, to provide an unconventional, yet accurate, description of penological practices from a perspective that isn't obstructed by political correctness.

The perils concerning the activities needed for the accomplishment of this goal are myriad. Prison officials grimace at the notion of NOT blocking self-instruction amongst detainees. In the non-fiction section of prison libraries, a twenty-year-old copyright date is relatively up-to-date; access to computers and free usage of word processing software is as much of a reality as brothels are on celestial bodies. Convicts are not allowed to aggregate in anyway, so group interviews and discussions must follow guidelines akin to those once deployed along the Underground Railroad. Speaking out against prison authorities results in administrative attacks and disciplinary actions, so this entire book was written in secret as if it were Anne Frank's diary being hidden from the Gestapo.

Concerning the actual composition of this book's content, as with any work of extensive range that radically challenges the status-quo and disrupts the prevailing regime of truth, there are other hazards that must be considered. Writings that neglect or overlook too much, invite the indignation of snubbed institutions and individuals as well as charges of unfair selection of information in efforts to espouse ulterior motives or agendas. Literature that travels in the opposite direction— cumbersome, immensely descriptive, detailed, and overly thorough dissections— becomes nothing more than a presentation of records and statistics, weighty in documentation but quite light in essence and meaning. To the extent possible, I've avoided both ends of this spectrum.

Given the deplorable resources at my disposal, I expect my critics to squeal at what they believe is my failure to cite sufficient data in support of my positions. My primary response is to point out that data supporting my assertions is not available for the free or the incarcerated. As the ensuing text will clarify, data compilers tend to neglect non-traditional viewpoints such as my own, a problem that is compounded by poorly executed field observations conducted by dedicated social scientists. My secondary retort is to encourage my readers to prevent unproductive criticisms such as these from blocking the deliberation of expressive commentary and clouding the reception of what is obviously much-needed empirical knowledge.

Remaining aware of possible progress-hindering pitfalls was important to me throughout the construction of this literary framework. This awareness led to the careful conveyance of ideas, the authentic identification of misinformation, and the debunking, with painstaking precision, of closely guarded myths. Such applicable awareness kept me on my proverbial "toes." It allowed me to remain poised to deliver this razor-sharp edict which will slice through, instead of being dulled by, the myopic and dogmatic arguments presented by legislative oligarchs and proponents of mass incarceration.

A *Convict's Perspective* is both a flame that is to be held to the feet of penologists and penal system administrators and a rally cry that is to be yelled in the ears of a snoozing public. It is not only a scathing critique of prison management, but also a summoning, an enticement, and an invitation to transcend the status quo. It builds on the work of Michelle Alexander. It is positioned on the shoulders of the revolutionary Angela Davis. It is my proposal for change, my recommendation for improvement, a portion of my map for societal advancement and social evolution.

This book is meant to awaken the masses, to compel bureaucracies to honor their civic commitments, and to address abhorrent public performances such as those outlined by John P. Conrad in *The Right of Wrongdoers.* In 1987 Mr. Conrad stated that "prisoner's rights don't excite the public as a righteous cause." He proposed that "in the interest of both the prisoners, the employees of the prison, and the general public, every prisoner has a right to conditions that won't make him a worse man. We know how hard it is to help prisoners to become better men, and many penal authorities have given up too easily on that task. But whatever prisons do, they must not make men needlessly worse. As to that requirement, there can be no competition of rights. Those who believe in justice as the essential virtue of social institutions in a democracy, face only the difficulty of prodding prison bureaucracies into recognition of their plain duty. Every bureaucracy cares more about its survival than the performance of plain duties, and of few can this be said more surely than those charged with the administration of prisons. Only the continuous vigilance of an informed public can assure that survival requires performance of duty manifested in the observance of rights."

May all passionate freedom fighters heed my suggestions and pursue penal reform for the sake of our security, for the sake of our livelihoods, and most importantly, for the sake of the future leaders of America.

PART ONE

PENOLOGY, PRISON, AND THE GULF IN BETWEEN

INTRODUCTION

Sports broadcaster, political analyst, and geologist; these three occupations all have something in common, believe it or not. These professions are similar in a way that is both understood and accepted by society at large. This similarity pertains to the level of expertise needed to perform in these professions. In other words, occupants of these vocations are alike in that they are each considered experts in their particular industry or field of study. They have an authoritative and often well-respected voice regarding their specific frames of reference.

Sports broadcasters are often former athletes who once possessed considerable skill and talent applicable to their sport of choice. As broadcasters, they attend sporting events, observe, interview, and actively interact with current athletes on and off the field or court, as well as stay abreast of rule changes, sporting records, injuries, trends, salaries, and up-and-coming athletic phenoms. A vast majority of political analysts were once employed by a public official and/or administration. They mingle and associate with current and former politicians, regularly consulting and evaluating giants within lively political arenas. Their assessments and opinions are quite influential due to their public associations with political "insiders." Geologists, more frequently than not, explore, study, and examine rock formations as they appear and occur in natural environmental settings. Historians, excavators, environmentalists, and even astronomers take counsel from geologists because they respect the specified knowledge, experience, and intensive academic preparation that geologists possess and undergo concerning history as it is recorded in rocks.

There's another group of professionals, however, that isn't as involved with its subjects as sports broadcasters, political analysts, and geologists tend to be: criminologists. These professionals, despite being unfairly prevented from engaging their subjects in the most effective manner, are also regarded as the experts of their field of criminology. *Merriam-Webster's Collegiate Dictionary, Eleventh Edition*, defines criminology as "the scientific study of crime as a social phenomenon, of criminals, and of penal treatment." The latter of these will be the focal point around which this book will revolve. More specifically as it is applied to "penal-related criminology," which I define here as the application of criminological knowledge, theory, and methods to the solution of specific penal-oriented problems. This applied penal-related criminology will be referred to as "penology" from this point forward.

It's worth noting that neither criminologists nor penologists can observe, examine closely, or accurately report on the behavior of current criminals or inhabitants of the penal system. This is due to fundamental inadequacies that are sprinkled throughout their limited methods of gathering data. Neither criminology nor penology, as fields of inquiry, have yet to encroach upon and assess the behavioral and mental tendencies of current inmates and career criminals in a meaningful, paradigm-shifting way. This is mainly because the subjects cannot be observed behaving naturally and because the means of research rely upon inaccurate and misleading information.

In this literary work, I will address an often ignored shortcoming. This growth-hindering shortcoming concerns the ways in which criminologists and penologists conduct research. I aim to expose the proverbial ball-and-chain that is shackled to the academic ankles of all who have chosen to delve into scholastic penology in the traditional sense. This ball-and-chain severely hinders criminological experts in their area of expertise. I will also expound on select incarceration-related matters from the perspective of an articulate detainee. This perspective is not only overlooked and underutilized by penologists, but also completely absent from academia and other intellectual arenas.

However, my goal is not to deprive penology of its legitimacy nor invalidate the time and energy that criminologists invest into educating themselves. My goal is to lend a hand to an underappreciated profession that studies and seeks to actualize current and potential methods of prisoner reformation as a means of crime reduction. My book aims to complement the ways in which research is conducted and interpreted. It's a necessary complement due to the restricted performance of research and its contribution to the current state of misdirection concerning the reduction of recidivism.

My findings and conclusions will begin the process of re-steering penal system administrators, legislators, bureaucrats, and educators toward more realistic goals and more effective methods of accomplishing these goals. I seek to contribute to the American Society of Criminology and the American Correctional Association, as well as to think tanks such as Right on Crime (spearheaded by the likes of Newt Gingrich, Geaver Norquist, and Ed Meese), the Smart and Safe Campaign, Smart on Crime, the Center for Impact Research, and individual penologists and criminologists (such as Dr. Jaime Vaske of Western Carolina University). These individuals, initiatives, and organizations can be enhanced, actualized, and more productively applied if crime promotion and recidivism is more sharply critiqued and better understood within the context of inmate reformation.

The following written observations and theorizations will be presented within this context. They will also be rooted in my own personal experiences as the human property of the North Carolina Department of Public Safety/Division of Adult Correction. These experiences, when thoughtfully analyzed, should contribute to all criminological fields of study.

CHAPTER 1:
Flaws in Penological Field Observation

"They are strangers to our character, ignorant of our capacity, oblivious to our history and progress, and are misinformed as to the principles and ideas that control and guide us as [inmates]. The great mass of American citizens estimates us as being a characterless and purposeless people; and hence we build up overheads, if at all, against the withering influence of a nation's scorn and contempt."

-*Frederick Douglass*
July 1853 (insertion mine)

Escorted Tours: Penologists tend to conduct studious inquiries and examinations of penal treatment (and its resulting effects) in one of three ways. Their pursuit and interpretation of facts, as well as their revisions of accepted theories in light of these facts, is guided by a triad of research methods. The first method addressed here is field observation.

Penologists conduct field observation to gather information about penitentiaries. This usually involves an escorted tour of a particular prison. On these tours, which I've witnessed on numerous occasions at multiple prisons, the "tourist" (i.e. the field-observing penologist) is escorted around the particular compound by a high-ranking administrative official— usually the facility's superintendent— as well as a high ranking uniformed officer— usually a captain or a lieutenant. Witnessing these tours as an inmate is actually sort of weird.

Prisoners freeze in silence like a bunch of deer staring into a convoy of headlights. They examine the escorts and the tourists and silently wonder how the aftermath of the tour will impact their lives. The "tourists," meanwhile, whisper amongst themselves and pretend to not notice the weirdness that surrounds them. The prison officials— escorts— stand back and watch what transpires while praying that an inmate doesn't take it upon himself to interrupt the proceedings. It's such a strange occurrence, that most of the people involved overlook the fact that allowing extremely disconnected escorts to be prison guides is the reason that the onset of observatory activities is tainted and misleading. This strangeness clouds their judgment.

Prison tourists/observers get hoodwinked by these escorts at every turn. They're never told that these escorts, administrative officials, and high-ranking uniformed officers receive all of their information concerning the prison's day-to-day operation from their subordinates— the correctional officers. The tour guides rarely, sometimes never, place themselves amongst the general inmate population to witness, firsthand, prison social mechanisms at work.

In the prison at which I'm currently being held are hundreds of inmates that don't even know the superintendent's name, let alone what he looks like or where his office is located. Prison observers basically have tour guides who know little more about prison life and circumstances than the observers themselves. The individuals that are more informed regarding prison social structures— i.e. prison residents— are often threatened into silence. (Harsh punishment is sometimes administered to inmates that attempt to converse with observers or inspectors with the intent of revealing certain deplorable, yet well-concealed, conditions.)

Sometimes, when prison administrators learn of an upcoming tour or inspection, the rowdy inmates are placed in the "hole" (solitary confinement). They're forced to wait in very tiny cells while the "tour" is taking place amongst the general inmate population. They are released from the hole once the tour is complete. Consequently, the observers are left with a false, misguided, and blurry view of the prison, a view given to them by tour guides who themselves could benefit from a *real* guided tour. It's akin to a space alien asking me to give him a tour of the White House on Pennsylvania Avenue. It's true that I live on the same planet and in the same country as the White House, and I even visited it when I was thirteen. Therefore, I may have more personal White House experience than the previously mentioned space alien, but in no way am I remotely qualified to be a White House tour guide. In the same way superintendents, captains, and lieutenants are not qualified to be prison tour guides. Superintendents especially make rare appearances among the general inmate population. When the word spreads of a superintendent's upcoming visit to a housing unit, inmates are forced to clean, scrub, sweep, mop, polish, and shine all visible surfaces. These officials don't even know what a real prison dorm looks like, let alone how it functions.

Beyond the unqualified tour guides and the temporary relocation of the more rowdy inmates, there are other procedural aspects of field (prison) observation that deserve further scrutiny and analysis.

Inmate Behavioral Adjustments:

Another common practice that I've witnessed while observing "prison tours" pertains to the way prisoners knowingly taint data collection methods. Many tourists try to observe inmates in their "natural habitat," and then they collect data by taking notes and documenting what they believe are inmates' normal activities (at least the activities of the chosen inmates that unqualified tour guides allow the "tourists" to see). A few inmates have told me that they were once randomly selected to be questioned by a touring penologist who was on a reconnaissance mission, like a CIA spy. These inmates told me that this undercover penologist/spy carefully analyzed their responses to certain questions; verbal and nonverbal communicatory behaviors such as body language, tone of voice, hand gestures, eye contact (or lack thereof), grammar usage, posture, and hygienic condition were all thoroughly noted.

Although I've never been personally interrogated by a penologist, I have seen tourists watching us, taking extensive notes, and photographing us as well as our living quarters. According to penological literature, these techniques are used to examine the ways in which inmates interact with staff members as well as amongst themselves.

I've never witnessed the fruit of these data collection methods, but I've witnessed the promotion of immorality; I've witnessed the denial of education; I've witnessed the endorsement of criminality and the destruction caused by constant recidivism. Simply put, I've witnessed the things that these tourists (penologists) should be combating and I am convinced that there is tremendous room for improvement.

To begin with, I must clearly state that inmates act and speak differently when non-inmates are watching. As a prison "insider" I've seen the ways in which inmates adjust their language and behavior when ANY outside presence is detected in the form of physical beings, cameras, microphones, etc. Detainees often try to speak and behave in a way that leads observers to believe their speech and behavior is that of a prisoner that isn't aware he's being observed. The very presence of penologists (or any other non-inmate) makes prisoners adjust themselves in a way that compromises the integrity of penologists' field observations. The knowledge that inmates are being monitored, as well as the ensuing "show"— the beguiling behavioral displays put on by the inmates— are variables of tremendous significance that aren't being accounted for.

Only prisoners themselves are privy to the deeper oracles of inmate behavior and prison life. If a penologist decides to study North Carolina's prisons and then ignores this important fact, his or her observations will be...well...*wrong*. And any hypothesis developed from these distorted and unknowingly falsified observations will be inaccurate. This *wrongness* and inaccuracy currently plagues modern day penology, and it's not the fault of the penologists. These individual penologists observe and report on what is wrongly presented to them as the regularity of detainee behavior, and then they develop models based on these observations and reports. They, along with other researchers, believe they are being extensive and thorough while they conduct penal experiments at various correctional institutions. However, they're unaware of the fact that the aforementioned flaws and inefficiencies are system-wide. This unawareness is part of the reason that the current models continue to accomplish very little.

Ignorance of Prison Culture:

Admittedly, given their position as what inmates perceive as outsiders, one cannot help but recognize and admire the penologists' dedication to traditional methods of conducting sociological field observations. Such dedication is admirable even if their efforts are tainted by their limited perspectives combined with the institution's deceptive tendencies.

Yet, there remains another unknown variable that prevents penologists from obtaining accurate and germane data. This variable is the prison's inhabitants, the very objects of study and observation. Throughout distant and recent history, any prison outsider that has attempted to analyze, examine, and accurately describe or report on the behavioral tendencies and psychological make-up of the incarcerated has failed. This succession of failures is due largely to the fact that prison's "culture" is mostly ignored; its significance regarding the social and psychological conditions of detainees is downplayed at the expense of gathering momentous data. (This term "culture" applies quite well in this context; I, however, use it with much caution and trepidation mainly because I'm aware of theoretical deformities that have originated from its overly ambiguous usage in past studies of crime and delinquency. As my readers will note, I've avoided such cloudy applications of this term.) This cultural ignorance, the fact that penologists "are misinformed as to the principles and ideas that control and guide us" as inmates, is calamitous concerning sociological data collection.

Professional sociologists should rarely attempt to study the actions of a particular people without first canvassing their culture. Doing so will only result in erroneous and misleading information. For example, in the American culture, maintaining a reasonable level of eye contact throughout an interaction is a sign of respect. It shows that each party is attentive to, and engaged in, what is being discussed or exchanged. Eye contact may even convey shamelessness or an admirable lack of fear.

This interpretation, however, is not universal. There are cultures that view extensive eye contact in a completely different light. What Americans view as an acceptable amount of eye contact, is sometimes interpreted otherwise (often as a sign of disrespect) in many other cultures. If a social scientist decides to scrutinize one of these other cultures without considering such cultural factors, he or she may wrongly conclude that the culture of study is full of inattentive, shameful, and fearful individuals.

The concept of detailed cultural recognition seems sensible. Most people familiar with sociology and anthropology understand that detailed and descriptive ethnographies are vital when it comes to contemplating differences and similarities between varying groups of people. Historical anthropologist Gerald Sider once wrote "...we can have no significant understanding of any culture unless we also know the silences that were institutionally created and guaranteed along with it..."

Nowhere is this observation more relevant in American society than in an analysis of the culture of mass imprisonment and long-term detention. Cultural ignorance seems to be widespread among criminologists who have chosen to research punitive institutions. It appears that they don't acknowledge the existence of a distinct prison culture— probably because they're fed so much crappy information. It's no wonder that, as a prison "insider," I tend to view their penological hypotheses and theorizations (the very best of which are rooted in phony ethnographies) as sardonic at best.

The Enculturation Process: Is

there a way for penologists to delve into the deeper recesses of prison culture? Is there a way for them to truly relate to a member of this unique "tribe"? There should be; don't you think? I, personally, expect penologists to scrutinize and understand each stage of the process that a prisoner goes through to become a member of the prison culture, as well as the resulting mental, emotional, and personality alterations. My expectations, however, do not seem to coincide with reality, and maybe this is because penologists just haven't found a "way."

Penology and criminology students have studied in depth the social and societal factors that often *precede* criminal behavior. Unfortunately, very few students expend sufficient amounts of energy on the way in which the first stage of this enculturation process affects a person's mind, and how crime commission impacts the perpetuator's psyche.

Consider "Leroy," my fellow inmate. Leroy committed a crime and got away with it for a little while. He ran, hid, ducked, and dodged the police for about a week after he broke the law. The act of eluding law enforcement personnel— albeit briefly— had a profound effect on Leroy's superego.

The act of committing the crime, followed by his avoidance of capture, gave Leroy a sense of "power," a sense of one-upmanship. He experienced this power as a triumph over what he viewed as an omnipotent and oppressive criminal justice system. The feeling that the system was being beaten, that Leroy had committed a crime and successfully avoided the monolithic hand of the law, translated into emotional success for him. More plainly put, Leroy considered the entire criminal justice system, especially law enforcement, as an antagonist. In his mind, outsmarting the antagonist meant that the criminal justice system was "losing," and he, the outsmarter who committed the crime and eluded the law, was "winning." This triumphant feeling was brand new for Leroy, and he liked it.

As a matter of fact, Leroy liked this feeling so much that he was engulfed by it. He allowed this feeling to hypnotize him because his entire life prior to it was a life of total powerlessness and social insignificance. To go from such a powerless state to a state of perceived triumph was a foreign, yet exhilarating, rush for Leroy. This was a rush of success, winning, and most importantly, power.

This new supposed power was quite euphoric and it translated into a sense of self-worth for Leroy. This euphoria heavily impacted his psyche and made the feeling of power more tremendous and lasting. It was sort of like a hit of psychological heroin for him. He became addicted to it, almost instantly.

Despite the intensity and duration of his euphoria, and regardless of however long his sense of one-upmanship lasted, it disappeared upon getting arrested and spending time as a pre-trial jail resident. When the police slapped those platinum bracelets (handcuffs) on Leroy's wrists, it served as a crushing blow to his psyche. In response, he immediately felt the urge to defend himself by countering this mental "blow." He fulfilled this urge by fighting authority figures in every way that he could think of— directly, indirectly, subtly, blatantly, whatever.

Having his "euphoric power" ripped away by the antagonist caused him to replace this power with two things: a hardened anti-authority sentiment and a desire to reclaim the power he was robbed of. Hating authority and yearning for power marked the beginning of Leroy's transformation into a member of the prison culture. To compound matters, Leroy was in jail at this point, surrounded by other power-hungry criminals. This means that he believed the only way to get power was by criminal means and everyone around him was eager to enforce this belief. When he looked within, he saw criminality. When he looked outward, he saw criminality. When he closed his eyes he heard almost eighty other Leroys spewing toxic criminality as if their mouths were lawless sewage pumps.

All of these "Leroys" were rewarded with power and significance for committing crimes and momentarily avoiding capture. Following behaviorist thinking, power and significance were akin to positive reinforcement. But as soon as these criminals are apprehended, this "power reward" is stripped away from them. The prison culture inductee doesn't view this inevitable deprivation of power (arrest and pre-trial detention) as the consequences of his actions. He doesn't see it as society's way of disciplining miscreants. The prison culture inductee views this deprivation of power as an unwarranted personal attack. He believes that getting arrested and having his new found power yanked away is just the criminal justice system's way of assaulting him; after all, isn't that what antagonists are suppose to do?

In the prison culture mindset, what is intended by law enforcement as discipline is interpreted as an unintelligible and undeserved assault. Psychiatric and psychological research has shown that such assaults— harsh, uncertain and unwarranted discipline— often lead to crime, instead of preventing it. Some experts even believe that the sense of powerlessness and insignificance that permeated most convict's pre-prison lives is a possible impetus to breaking the law.

Therefore, assaulting inmates in this way (giving them what they perceive as harsh, uncertain, and unwarranted discipline) and making them feel even more powerless and empty should not be the justice system's go-to move. This only creates more dedicated criminals who, at the beginning of their incarceration experience, are only exposed to the same conditions and mentalities that led to their incarceration in the first place. I know that prison culture inductees' interpretation of their arrest and their pre-trial confinement seems distorted and kind of twisted, but it is a very palpable reality in my world.

You must not forget that I'm writing this book from the inside. Not only do I know Leroy, I see him every day. I'm sitting beside a "Leroy" right now. There's another "Leroy" sweeping the floor, and a third "Leroy" using the telephone. There's a "Leroy" sleeping on the bunk behind me, while another "Leroy" is sitting across from me watching television. There are "Leroys" everywhere; I'm surrounded by them. Hell, I used to *be* a "Leroy." I went through the same power-chasing and power-deprivation stages. I managed to transcend them, but not before feeling like the system was unfairly attacking me.

When I lived as a pre-trial prisoner I became acutely aware of the tragic ways in which harsh and uncertain discipline can get more and more intense as time progresses. There were strip searches and intrusive viewings of my genitalia by complete strangers on a regular basis. (These searches were unavoidable because physical assault is the administrative remedy for any inmate who refuses to disrobe.) I saw my captors delay and destroy outgoing and incoming mail, deny visits and revoke phone privileges also. These uncalled for means of discipline dehumanized many detainees by further distancing them from their loved ones— the only people who were willing to confirm these guys' humanity.

Furthermore, being locked in a cell, alone, for twenty-three hours a day destroyed what little social capacities these detainees managed to hold on to. Also, heat pumped through these cells in the summer, and air conditioning blasted through them in the winter (painfully opposite of what's normal). This ruined many prisoners' ability to cope with and understand their physical confinement.

Not to mention the "cell extractions" that I basically begged to NOT be subjected to. Cell extractions are where officers, in groups of five— one for each body extremity— dress in riot gear and assault inmates for no apparent reason and then justify their actions with fabricated incident reports. Combine all of these things and it is a recipe for the demolition of prisoner's self-worth, self-respect, dignity, integrity, and most pertinent, their inclination to pursue habilation.

By the way, all of the above happens BEFORE a trial has occurred, BEFORE innocence or guilt has been proven. It is the beginning of the induction into the prison culture and already many severe social and psychological traumas have been inflicted; traumas that every current or former prisoner has endured with almost zero exceptions. These traumas tremendously alter psychological make-up and societal perceptions, and this alteration serves as a precursor to prison culture membership.

Unbelievably, the idea that overly harsh and ill-defined treatment is responsible for inmates not taking advantage of any habilitative programs, and instead leads to prisonization, seems to escape the administration. The people who are responsible for the implementation of reformative practices don't seem to realize that the very beginning of this cultural transformation process is terribly flawed.

In this stage of the transformation, the ways in which inmates define and satisfy their needs begin to differ dramatically from those of cultural outsiders (i.e. free people). Individuals in this stage of the enculturation process reside in a world whose social structure only vaguely resembles that of the free civilization. They live in an imprisoned society that consists of noticeably different communicatory inclinations, a significantly different form of currency, a vastly different description of how love and affection is displayed, and immensely different styles of clothing one's person. Their confined society also has a dangerously different method of obtaining "status," undeniably different means of conflict resolution, abstractly different customs and rituals, slightly different manners of religious observance, and drastically different valuations of entertainment. Awareness of these differences would combat the tendency to observe and assess the lives of prison's residents from a foreign and disconnected culture's viewpoint. I want penologists and other researchers to abandon this tendency and avoid viewing inmates through a lens fashioned to a free society's angle of refraction. This view produces a blurry and out of focus picture that leads some penologists to mistakenly support bad programs and theories. This support and the already established social, emotional, and psychological influences (attacks) only push pre-trial detainees deeper and deeper into the crime-friendly prison culture (it's like strapping cinderblocks to the ankles of someone who has just dived into the "prison culture pool").

The effects of this pre-trial detention stage are even more poignant when you factor in the detainee's acceptance of powerlessness concerning his future. Let's consider Leroy again. During his pre-trial confinement, he not only realized that his future was quite uncertain, but he also learned that he could do nothing to change this uncertainty. Leroy discovered that judicial titans (alleged agents of criminal justice) were going to be determining what his future would and would not consist of, and this discovery forced him to come to grips with the fact that he would be completely excluded from this decision-making process.

Understanding that a handful of individuals— with whom he's never conversed nor interacted— would be making upcoming major life decisions FOR him, served as a moment of clarity for Leroy. It caused him to clearly see how very little he controlled. It caused him to accept his powerlessness. And knowing that he couldn't control his immediate nor distant future, in turn, diminished Leroy's ability to exercise foresight. It caused him to focus entirely on the one thing that he believed he could still control— the present.

Inmates in this situation devote the bulk of their attention to the "right here" and the "right now" because they believe everything else is out of their hands. This devotion exponentially intensifies impulsiveness

(impulsiveness and a lack of foresight being the primary reasons most inmates are incarcerated in the first place).

From this perspective, it is easy to see that this system, established for the so-called purpose of ridding society of crime and ensuring public safety, is actually nourishing and promoting criminous character flaws. Once an individual embraces these and other criminal tendencies encouraged by the penal system, once a person is completely infected by the virus known as "prison" and has prison culture lodged into him, it is very difficult to expunge. The virus persists, but it is not fatal; the patient survives but is never whole.

Inmate Outlook: These four stages of
the enculturation/prison culture infection process (crime commission, elusion of law enforcement, the arrest, and the pre-trial detention) lead to the creation of a culturally new individual. The life of this culturally new detainee will consist of little more than personally significant, yet societally insignificant, efforts aimed at recapturing the power that was tasted during the first and second stages. This psychological orientation, this poorly conceived "power chase," is both encouraged by the prison system and ignored by habilitation advocates. What shocks me the most about this reality is its uniformity. It occurs in approximately the same way for every prison culture inductee. A teenaged black kid who likes crack-cocaine and idolizes Suge Knight, and a middle-aged white man with a marketing degree and an eagerness to quote Ronald Reagan as much as possible will meet the same prison culture fate. This is probably because of the justice system's intense efforts to deprive its prey of individuality.

By this, I mean, the "distinctiveness theory" is the only concept pertaining to prison's psychological effects that the architects of this penal system have ever considered, and even it is being applied unproductively. This theory holds that people define themselves according to what makes them different from others in a particular context. In *Advances in Experimental Social*

Psychology, William J. and Claire V. McGuire elaborate on this by stating that "...one perceives oneself in terms of characteristics that distinguish oneself from other humans, especially from people in one's usual social milieu...a woman psychologist in the company of a dozen women who work at other occupations thinks of herself as a psychologist. When with a dozen male psychologists she thinks of herself as a woman."

With this theory in mind, I bet you can imagine the effects of the penal system. It is structured in a way that severely restricts the ways in which inmates can distinguish themselves from the lawless and anti-authoritarian status quo. Excessive resources are allocated for the purpose of maintaining this status quo and actualizing widespread uniformity. Not only do inmates wear the same clothes and the same style shoes, but a 120 pound inmate is served the same amount (and variety) of food as a 320 pound inmate. Inmates also reside in identical living quarters and sleep on identical twin-sized mattresses regardless of their height disparities.

Moreover, inmates are given access to the same kinds of intellectually oriented resources irrespective of their intellectual differences, and they are allowed to only use these resources in a shallow and uniform manner. They are even disciplined in the same way when policies or rules are violated regardless of their blatantly different learning styles. Inmates also share the same toilets, sinks, and showers, and at some facilities inmates are required to wear identical closely cropped hairstyles and adorn a predetermined amount of facial hair.

Most penal system architects endorse this systematic obsession with "sameness." They believe that most people respect the law, adhere to the law, and don't believe that they can get away with breaking the law. They also believe criminals are the ones that step outside of this and adopt the belief that the law doesn't apply to them as individuals.

These prison architects — proclaimers of the "individuality-causes-crime" idea— believe that in order to correct criminal tendencies, criminals must be taught to conform. They must reject or be deprived of what these penal designers view as negative individuality. They must learn that they're just like everyone else when it comes to law-abiding citizenship. Combine this belief—manifested through the removal of inmate differences—with the premise that people define themselves based on their differences, and one question arises: How does one define oneself if he's just like everyone else? (Upon considering conformity, an additional question arises: How can one be taught to conform to lawful cultural standards if one is kept in prison and never exposed to nor informed of such standards?)

For these architects to believe that criminals commit crimes because of their individuality, and that eliminating individuality and promoting conformity and "sameness" is the key to reducing crime, they must ignore certain criminogenic facts. More specifically, they must turn a blind eye towards the reality that most so-called criminals grow up in environments thronged with people that are similar to them. The fact that they lack relative individuality and are often unable to distinguish themselves from their crime-loving peers is probably why they live a life of crime in the first place. More plainly put, if an individual is surrounded by criminals and the ways in which he distinguishes himself from these criminals are non-existent, he'll eventually come to believe that he is just like these other criminals to a certain extent, whether it's true or not. What if this individual is just a sixteen-year-old minor that made a bad decision that landed him in prison? He'll learn nothing from incarceration except that he is a criminal.

In such a scenario, the criminal justice system once again effectively CREATES a criminal that society will eventually demonize for displaying criminal behaviors, a demonization that will only further embed criminality into this individual. In other words, prior to incarceration this individual is thoroughly indoctrinated with criminality. He's then sent to prison as punishment for acting on his indoctrination, and this "punishment" deepens his belief that criminality is his only option in life.

But even though further brainwashing will ironically be his punishment for being brainwashed, he will still remain completely human. His primary identity will not be that of a father, a student, an executive, a politician, an entrepreneur, or a civil servant; it will be that of a man living in a modern society. Upon his release, and despite viewing himself chiefly as a criminal or as a "gansta," he will not stop trying to do his own version of what modern, civilized humans do— excel. He will still chase excellence and pursue means of enhancing his identity for the same reasons as most Americans— for success, a sense of purpose, a sense of meaning, and most importantly, for power.

His pursuit, however, is deeply criminous; it's painted with the brush of chronic illegality. His destination is the same as that of most people, but his route is the road of lawlessness. This personally significant pursuit of "power" and of "excellence" (which is frowned upon by society because of the criminous "road" on which this pursuit takes place) will eventually lead him back to prison where the cycle will be repeated and where criminality will be reinforced. With hopes of maintaining a sense of personhood, a sense of humanity, a sense of intrinsic value and substantiveness— these senses being previously defined as power— the inmate will partake in many acts of rebellion, such as not obeying authority figures when orders are given, and challenging authority figures whenever the opportunity to do so presents itself.

To summarize, let's throw Leroy back into the mix. Before confinement Leroy was rewarded with what he perceived as power after committing a crime and evading punishment for a certain amount of time. Then he was stripped of this power as soon as he was arrested, a stripping which Leroy interprets as an unjustified attack. Next, pre-trial detention completely altered Leroy's self-perception and societal outlook for the worse. He embraced impulsiveness, personal insignificance, his lack of foresight, and what became an all-encompassing sense of criminality.

Incarceration infected him, and this infection left him with just two options: either be sent from jail to prison, or be released only to return shortly thereafter for giving in to his criminous impulses. Either way, further or additional confinement was inevitable, and so was the hardening of anti-authority sentiments within Leroy's character. He now has no doubt that authority figures are antagonists who are consistently trying to re-strip him of power, to figuratively (or sometimes literally) re-arrest him.

A major portion (upwards of ninety percent) of the prison culture is composed of people that think and perceive in this manner. They view life as one continuous power struggle and nothing more. To them, life is not something to be enjoyed and cherished. In their eyes, life is not an interesting tapestry of fates progressing beautifully. Life, for them, is something to be struggled through and sometimes fought against— albeit unconsciously. This perception is what determines their actions and behaviors as detainees.

Myopic Experts: It isn't appropriate to use culturally irrelevant criteria to diagnose the possessors of this "prison perception." I have made this pretty clear. Unfortunately, many penologists are inclined to do this very thing. This inclination is quite perplexing to me, especially when I consider the trend towards cultural relativism that began to gain speed in the twentieth century amongst social scientists. A cultural relativist named Frank Boas was at the forefront of this trend. He really highlighted the need for dispassionate and objective descriptions of any people that sociologists choose to assess. He understood how essential it was/is for social scientists to strive to prevent their own cultural values from coloring the descriptive accounts of any people under study.

Knowing this, I must admit that it bothers me when I encounter penologists who seem to have failed to follow suit. Their work directly impacts my life when they endorse poor policies, so it's troubling when they appear to completely ignore the existence of a prison subculture, or when they abide by the notion that their own culture possesses a set of absolute standards by which all other cultures can be judged. I've heard the argument that these missteps are the reasons why this society has yet to reduce the recidivism rate by any significant amount.

It's not my goal to place such a tremendous weight on the shoulders of these capable academics, but I can't help but ponder on this argument when it's presented. Could the cultural arrogance of penologists really be why prisons create crime moreso than reduce it? Could the selective and consequently defective perspective of penologists really be hindering positive prison system evolution? And why is inmate reform the only field that seems to be plagued by this "selective" perspective?

Criminologist Stanley Cohen wrote a book called *State of Denial* that comes to mind when I attempt to debate the answers to these questions. In this book, Cohen examined how individuals and institutions know about, yet deny, the occurrence of criminally oppressive acts. He claimed that people see only what they want to see and wear blinders to avoid seeing the rest. This is, and has been true about slavery, genocide, torture, and every other form of systemic oppression and neglect including penal system operations and inmate reform. But if this is known, why do people continuously fail to acknowledge criminogenic penal systems? If this has been documented and examined by a respected academic, why do penologists continue to wear blinders that block their views of prison culture? And even when the prison culture is acknowledged by penologists, why aren't these acknowledgements changing the policies that protect the justice system's flaws?

Many criminologists are on the right side of this issue (shout out to Joan Petersilia), but it's not enough of them to truly make the existence of the prison culture common knowledge. I will not attempt to give reasons why this is so. I will, however, note that a lack of concern for making the emic approach to prison culture more popular could possibly explain the absence of models and theories that have led, or will lead to the reformation of convicted criminals on a large scale.

Most penologists are very intelligent individuals, but sometimes this intelligence is not enough to combat what mainstream American culture teaches its members about those who break the law. Despite their impressive capabilities and humanitarian spirits, sometimes they can't help but hold progress-hindering ideas about convicts in the back of their minds— ideas that stem from judging convicted lawbreakers by inapplicable cultural standards. And it's astonishing how impactful those dormant ideas can be.

In *The Clash of Civilizations: Remaking of World Order,* Samuel P. Huntington touched on this issue in a very eloquent way. He wrote that " [s]implified paradigms or maps are indispensable for human thought and action. On the one hand, we may explicitly formulate theories or models and consciously use them to guide our behavior. Alternatively, we may deny the need for such guides and assume that we will act only in terms of specific *objective* facts, dealing with each case *on its merits.* If we assume this, however, we delude ourselves. For in the back of our minds are hidden assumptions, biases, and prejudices that determine how we perceive reality, what facts we look at, and how we judge their importance and merits," (emphasis in the original text).

This last sentence is of supreme importance because it applies so acutely to the way that those labeled as criminals are viewed and classified. But sadly, there are no paradigms that account for what is hidden in the back of penologists' minds. Worse yet, there are no behavioral guides for those that research inmate reform mainly due to the ignorance (or discrediting) of prison culture. For a penologist to ignore the "free-society-culture-to-prison-culture" transformation that every prisoner undergoes to a certain degree is to jeopardize any and all research conducted on punitive institutions and their residents. The work of these underappreciated scholars is much too valuable to not take root because of mere oversights and lack of access to more organic information. I, as well as other Incarcerated Thinkers, want them to use our insight and take post-crime commission enculturation into account when they conduct field observations. We want them to make these considerations so that they can effectively and accurately translate their findings into useful data and techniques that can be applied to the habilitation of convicts.

It will behoove all parties if we remind penologists of the fact that the United States is a pluralistic society composed of various subcultures, the prison subculture being one of pertinence to their field. Communities everywhere will benefit greatly if penologists pursue crime reduction with this in mind. Just as free mainstream American subcultures are mostly centered around various forms of liberty, autonomy, and success, the prison culture revolves around anti-authoritarianism and the obtainment of power to varying extents.

This unique orientation, this mental focal point amongst convicts, is extremely weighty and past reformative programs and initiatives have failed to the extent that this orientation has been marginalized or completely neglected. This book is meant to remind penologists that future program and/or initiatives must have a structure that accounts for this orientation or they too will fail to be effective.

CHAPTER 2:
A Complement to Traditional Penological Field Observation

"I, for one, believe that if you give people a thorough understanding of what confronts them and the basic causes that produce it, they will create a program, and when the people create a program you get action."

—El-Hajj Malik El-Shabazz

Some detainees have simply accepted the flawed field observatory methods of penologists as a given. They believe that penologists can't help but rush through their craft, as if they can't hold off on making evaluations until more accurate facts are known. There are even some radical Incarcerated Thinkers that believe these academics cannot suppress their egos and let go of old paradigms, nor can they loosen their grip on their sense of cultural certainty, even if their careers depended on it. These radical Incarcerated Thinkers have also repeatedly revealed to me three beliefs that they cling to— while reminding me that they have yet to come across anything that disproves these beliefs: 1) penological experts don't want to learn how prisoners view non prisoners; 2) penologists are unwilling to see the internal logic of the prison culture mindset; and 3) it is impossible for penologists to understand fully the components of prison culture without complete immersion, an immersion that is quite unlikely to happen because it can only occur to people that have been charged with criminal malfeasance.

Although I do not completely agree with all of these beliefs, I must admit that this latter belief possesses a kernel of truth. Penologists cannot live in prison in the same way that other experts in other subsets of sociology can live with their people of study; unlike other sociological subdivisions, penologists simply cannot reside in the community (i.e. prison) on which they intend to conduct research. For this reason, they shouldn't rely on the typical sociological version of field observation.

If they do rely on this insufficient means of collecting information, it will not enable them to formulate accurate descriptions of, and explanations for, the observed behavior of the incarcerated. Leaning heavily on such flawed field observatory techniques tends to restrict penological research. It also seems to cloud the fact that convicts know much more about penologists, than penologists know about convicts. Obscuring this fact serves as a "research-restriction supercharger" which further hinders the gathering of information. I've yet to read any penological literature that accounts for the fact that inmates are fully aware of both the cultural mechanisms of penologists as well as the ways in which penologists perceive them. If such literature does exist, it has been unfairly marginalized and pushed aside. This must change. To be effective, researchers must know what inmates know. They must know that inmates can, and often do, adjust themselves according to a particular image that they wish to display when they're being observed— while penologists being misinformed about prison culture remain unaware of said adjustments.

Don't get me wrong here; I'm not saying that academics are complete failures because they don't seem to know the intricacies of prison culture. They sometimes make positive contributions to the lives of inmates that are passionately pursuing personal and societal advancement despite their lack of authentic knowledge. (For example, anthropologist Elizabeth Grobsmith served as a cultural broker on behalf of Native American inmates in Nebraska to ensure the recognition of Native American religious ceremonies as legitimate.)

What I am saying is that penologists, and, in turn, their human objects of study, may possibly benefit from a more sincere application of functionalism to their methods of research. This means that their research-related activities should reflect an acceptance of the fact that no matter how strange, harmful, or seemingly counterproductive an item or action within the prison culture might at first appear, it has a meaning and performs what is perceived as some useful function for the individual or for the prison culture as a whole (a function that can only truly be defined and clarified by prison "natives").

There are some social scientists committed to studying the lives of the incarcerated that need to redirect their focus. These scholars should concentrate on identifying the mental and social structures that undergird the social behavior of detention residents. Instead of arrogantly thinking they can interpret, define, and give meaning to the lives of members of the prison culture, they should take a more descriptive (and less definitive) approach to their discipline by examining how the inmates themselves interpret their own values and behaviors. I don't think that it's too far-fetched to acknowledge that cultures can best be understood by listening and recording the ways in which the members themselves (more specifically the members that are willing to provide, and capable of generating, detailed articulations) explain their own customary behavior.

This opinion of mine, however, has not caught on within the domain of penology. The prison system keeps both novices and veterans of this field away from Incarcerated Thinkers, and this prevents penologists' from truly learning about the prison culture. As a result, inmates tend to get classified according to broad, oversimplified, and inapplicable laws and models which are aimed at predicting inmate behavior. All the while, the more advanced prison culture inductees get muzzled for trying to announce the uncomfortable truth, which is that these laws and models ignore the complexity and living qualities of prison culture and its individual members.

This arrangement keeps penologists bound to a monocultural approach when studying punitive facilities. And what is most puzzling is that only prison-related research seems to be approached in this fashion. Every other social science is approached from a variety of cultural vantage points, but not penology. A friend once told me that this special treatment means that penal system researchers are either ignorant of prison culture's significance or they purposely ignore it. I leaned more towards the former; he leaned more towards the latter (he sort of attributed penology's special treatment to the negative stigma that inmates are saddled with).

In *Culture and Conduct* (1991), Richard Barrett captured the essence of my friend's position. He addressed the importance of NOT ignoring the perspective when he claimed that it enables social scientists "...to view the world through two or more cultural lenses at once. They can thus think and perceive in the categories of their own cultures, but are able to shift gears, so-to-speak, and view the same reality as it might be perceived by members of the [cultures] they have studied." When I read this, it verified that the multicultural approach to research isn't completely foreign to all social scientists. It also made me question why this approach isn't apparent when exploring the work of certain criminologists and other purveyors of penal reform.

The answer to this question may stem from the notion that very few penologists believe the prison culture actually exists. This may be a radical stance, but I must address it here because...well...I feel like it.

It's really quite easy for someone in my situation to take this radical stance. Here in prison, this stance isn't even radical, it's moderate. I've met a few Incarcerated Thinkers who've adopted this "moderate" position. They think that I've given practicing penologists too much credit by claiming that they are merely misinformed about a few things, instead of flat out *uninformed* about everything.

And now that I think about it, complete and utter ignorance would account for the absence of a multicultural approach to penology. Being totally unaware of the fact that the prison culture is an American subculture would explain many penological missteps. (Examples of other American subcultures are the informal "Flower Child" culture that originated in the 1950s and 1960s, the "Hip-Hop" culture that the 1980s gave birth to, and both the modern day "Gothic" culture and the self-professed "Skateboard" culture.) If the majority of penologists don't view the prison culture as substantive, then penology as a field of study would not reflect accurate prison culture mechanisms— as it currently does not. Of the handful of penologists that would inevitably view the prison culture as something real, most would also believe that the prison culture should acculturate. They would believe that more cultural diffusion should be occurring. And sadly, they would likely dismiss the prison culture once they realized that it's not acculturating and that it isn't becoming what they believe it should be.

As an aspiring convict criminologist, I must partially agree with their belief. In private discussions, I often state emphatically that inmates, with help from prison administrators, should be striving to make prison culture more accurately reflect the law-abiding culture of the free society. I also maintain that reformation and habilitation will occur to the extent that this is accomplished.

I, however, strongly oppose the practice of dismissing the prison culture simply because it isn't what it should be. Empirically speaking, expecting the prison culture to mirror that of our lawful and non-incarcerated society is quite a utopian expectation. The current social, intellectual, and cultural climate within penal systems (such as the North Carolina Department of Public Safety/Division of Adult Correction— Prisons) is quite unique, with very few parallels beyond prison walls. Such a utopian expectation is so distant from the current reality that framing rehabilitative programs on

53

this Shangri-la will only result in stagnant, if not increasing, recidivism rates and excessively high prison populations. Both of which currently exist primarily because of the ineffective and improperly framed reformative measures into which prisoners are continuously thrusted.

My overall point here is simple. Formally trained penal system experts need to be encouraged to acknowledge the prison culture and learn about it from its most advanced members. They should look at "inmate-ism" from not only their traditional vantage point, but from a much closer one as well — and no other vantage point is closer than that of the Incarcerated Thinkers. Penologists especially, should understand and apply the concept of listening to the input of capable detainees so that prison culture can be understood and dealt with according to a new and improved understanding. I believe that reformation within the prison culture will occur to the extent that this is accomplished, and to the extent that this contributes to a productive paradigm shift within the field of penology.

As S.P. Huntington wrote, "[i]ntellectual and scientific advances...consist of displacement of one paradigm, which has become increasingly incapable of explaining new or newly discovered facts [i.e. high recidivism rates and prison populations], by a new paradigm which does account for those facts in a more satisfactory fashion."

CHAPTER 3:
Flaws in Penological Statistical Studies

"Every system of control depends for its survival on the tangible and intangible benefits that are provided to those who are responsible for the system's maintenance and administration. This [prison] system is no exception."

—*Michelle Alexander*
The New Jim Crow: Mass Incarceration in the Age of Colorblindness

The second research method prevalent within the field of penology is known as "statistical studies." It is basically the use of "statistics" as a means of gathering data. More specifically, in the *World Book Encyclopedia, 2006 Edition: Volume Four*, it states that criminologists "use statistics to study the ...characteristics of criminals...Statistics help criminologists find relationships between crime...and certain physical or social conditions...Criminologists also use statistics to learn about personality traits or social conditions that are more common among criminals than other people." In certain regions there are penologists who focus solely on analyzing statistics and determining whether or not these stats support or disprove certain penological and criminological theories. It sounds like a very boring job, but someone has to do it because it's considered vital to the study of crime. The people that have these boring jobs tend to rely on a variety of mathematical operations: means, or arithmetic "averages," and the use of correlation coefficients (which indicate the degree of correlation between two sets of data or between two random variables) are just two examples amongst many. In fact, there are so many operations and formulas used by these statistically-oriented penologists that listing them all in this text would be a never-ending endeavor.

I don't want this book to be as lengthy as the Dead Sea Scrolls, so I've decided to limit my scope to two formulas in particular — standard deviation and variance. These two mathematical operations are used by penal researchers to illustrate how "spread out" their information is. Amongst the plethora of statistical measures and categorization techniques that are applied to these sorts of analyses, these two formulas are the most obvious and commonly used. What Michael Jackson was to pop music, standard deviation is to penal research; what Miley Cyrus did for twerking, variance did for statistical analyses. But unlike Michael and Miley, standard deviation and variance are most responsible for leading researchers down paths strewn with inaccuracies and misrepresentations.

Yet, before I address the damages for which these two formulas are liable, I must first expound on "self-regulating" prisons (i.e. the conveniently concealed fact that the prison system survives and thrives in spite of its inefficiencies because its administrators have the luxury of policing themselves). My explanation of penologists' statistical and data-processing miscarriages can be better understood if I begin by elaborating on how the very source of the data that is used by these penologists taints, clouds, and distort their pursuit of information.

Government Compilations of Statistics:

As my readers know, the use of statistics as a means of research is not exclusive to penology. Businesses, schools, campaigns, organizations, law enforcement agencies, and almost all subdivisions of sociology refer to statistics or compilations of survey results when critiquing a particular group of people. Intelligent political candidates sometimes rely on statistics compiled by right-leaning, left-leaning, non-partisan, for-profit, non-profit, grassroots, mainstream, economic, social, municipal and scholastic institutions, organizations, and companies. Statisticians will agree that getting data from such a diverse array of statistical sources is relatively wise when compared to the narrow-sighted alternative. And most regular folk can agree with this. I'll go a step further and say that any moderately intelligent individual knows that tapping into just one source would leave too much room for error and miscalculation.

If I were a Republican political candidate running for office, it would be disdainful for me to consider no other sources beyond Fox News. They likely would provide me with biased data because they proudly lean to the right side of most political issues. In doing research on the favorability of country music in America, it would be foolish for me to depend solely on information provided by the attendees of the annual Country Music Awards. The high likelihood that almost all of the attendees will have a favorable opinion of country music would obviously compromise the integrity of my research.

Likewise, in analyzing the effectiveness of a particular group of school teachers, it would be senseless for me to rely only on tests that were created, administered, and scored by the teachers themselves. They have a natural inclination to over-represent their teaching prowess by forewarning their students, providing their students with answers to the tests, or by doctoring tests results. This isn't the raw stuff that sound data is made of. To further illustrate my point, it would be a little stupid for marketing executives, in conducting market research, to lean entirely on any demographic assessments given to them by their primary competitor. This competitor may resort to deception and sabotage to get the upper hand and increase their bottom line.

This is easy to understand and quite agreeable. So much so, that I used to believe that all individuals that regularly refer to statistical data in efforts to reach a specific goal receive input from a variety of statistical sources. At the very least, I thought they consulted with an independent source that wasn't directly linked to the topic being studied, a source that didn't believe it was in their best interest to alter statistical data or misguide researchers.

I've been proven wrong over the years. It's now very obvious that my belief was never really reflective of reality, especially within the field of penology. Penologists are very competent in academics, but I've learned that their most utilized source of statistical data is as far from independent as one can be. This source is actually making penologists look bad, and they should really begin to question whatever this source tells them.

The previously quoted *Encyclopedia* identified this "source" in the following text: "[s]tatistics and other data sources used by penologists] generally are compiled by government agencies." The significance of this must not be disregarded considering the fact that an overwhelming majority of punitive establishments are owned by the taxpayers and managed by government officials. (In North Carolina there's only one prison whose status as private or public is questionable, but the remaining institutions— which number close to six dozen— are publically owned and government operated). This means that penologists use information provided by a taxpayer-owned institution to study that taxpayer-owned institution. This is self-policing at its finest! At the very least, what you have here is a government agency that is responsible for compiling the statistics that will be used to scrutinize and monitor itself and maybe its fellow agencies and sister establishments.

This practice of "self-policing" has rarely worked efficiently, if at all, throughout human history, and it obviously isn't working now. (It's debatable as to whether or not anyone would be aware of the absurdly high recidivism rate and lack of reformative progress behind prison walls without the few independent and non-governmental agencies that actually do seek to hold the government accountable on issues like this; very few of these nongovernmental agencies actually develop objective and unbiased data pertaining to criminal justice though. And progressive penologists simply don't have enough support to guard against the dangers of this self-policing practice.)

For instance, many inmates suffer injustices at the hands of prison administrators. Sometimes these administrators, in fits of emotional irresponsibility, violate not only institutional codes of conduct, but governmental policies and procedures along with state laws. In many of these instances, victimized detainees pursue legal remedies to the problematic abuse. The most relevant legal remedy is to sue someone or, more importantly, to sue state governmental departments.

However, the outcomes of these latter lawsuits against government agencies, outcomes which almost never favor the detainee, have been statistically documented and reported on by other government agencies. Consequently, these statistics have given many prison staff members a feeling of invincibility when it comes to the treatment of inmates. It pretty much goes like this: one governmental entity (the court system) policies another governmental entity (the prison system), and the former continuously justifies the wrongdoings of the latter by constantly dismissing claims of misconduct on shallow grounds.

This, in turn, causes the prison system to deem its own misconduct appropriate simply because its overseer (the court system) inadvertently claims that it is. The court system and the prison system are homeboys, so of course they want each other to look good. This translates into another failed self-policing application. The statistics that these dog-and-pony shows produce are reported according to the criminal justice system's best interests (not those of society at large), so they show that inmate lawsuits are often dismissed in a court of law. Resultingly, inmate claims of abuse are viewed as unfounded, the proverbial "crying wolf," so-to-speak, and they're therefore not taken seriously.

This idea was conveyed in a July 2012 article entitled "Institutionalized Mind: The Breaking Process," written by a federal prisoner and published in the *Under Lock and Key* newsletter. This federal prisoner wrote that "[t]here are over a thousand cited...cases of prisoner lawsuits dismissed as frivolous, or on some contrived technicality, e.g. failure to exhaust administrative remedies/the institutional grievance process, even when that "grievance process" affords no capacity for redress...Emboldened by success at having prisoner lawsuits dismissed, prison staff have become more abusive and more blatant. This abuse and torture has had the desired effect, and many prisoners stop reporting staff abuse and just accept it. Thus, happens the moral decay of the prison population. Men and women who were social pariahs when free...become scavengers who lack morals, integrity, and principles. Human beings are confined and allow the conditions of that confinement to make them into predatory beasts...In America's prisons, what morals and integrity that is left in the prisoner is slowly eroded away. Those who never used alcohol become drunks on prison-made wine; those who never used drugs become heroin addicts with self-made needles; psychotropic medication babies; gunners— flashing and masturbating in front of prison staff."

This excerpt captures an underlying sentiment that permeates prison culture. This sentiment is an aversion to cronyism. Better yet, it is an allergy to cronyism. As an inmate, I must say that I'm not alone in denouncing the cronyism that saturates the criminal justice system. All inmates loathe it, and most have been harmed by it when it reared its ugly face. The most common form that this ugly face takes is the form of "self-policing" injustices.

Governmental statistics— pertaining to inmate abuse and lawsuits— that are given to penological researchers continuously herd these researchers towards discrediting the frequency and the intensity of the physical, emotional, mental, and criminogenic abuse that's often dished out by prison staff. This is cronyism at its proudest moment and it's deeply infused into the criminal justice system. Social cronyism is the culprit when criminal courts avidly adhere to the notion that police officers infallibly carry out their duties as law enforcement personnel. It serves as the foundation of the belief that anyone that's arrested and brought before the court is a guilty criminal and deserves to be treated as such. (Lie detector tests are a major part of this foundation. They are viewed as flawless in spite of the fact that anxiety causes the same physiological responses as deception. Consider that no records exist that document a lie detector machine indicating a falsehood when someone admitted to a crime; individuals are only believed when they admit to a crime, not when they deny it, regardless of what the machine detects.)

Prison officials, likewise, immerse the court system in a pool of perfection. They seem to believe that the courts would not unfairly or unjustly send someone to prison; therefore, all inmates deserve to be treated like the societal scum that they're perceived to be. Some prison officials don't realize that mistreatment and punishment of inmates isn't their responsibility, that just being in prison itself is the punishment. This is a product of their perception of the court system.

The prison thinks the court is perfect; the court thinks that police are perfect; and the police view all ex-convicts as bad people, as if the prisons where they once lived did right by holding them behind bars as long as they did. To compound matters, when an individual opposes or challenges any of these false perceptions he or she is immediately vilified, discredited, and disregarded by all of these entities combined.

This social cronyism operates alongside the criminal justice system's financial cronyism. Note the Second Chance Act (SCA) and its pathetic record. The SCA, signed into law by G.W. Bush in 2008, was intended to help former prisoners find jobs, reintegrate into society, and avoid recidivism. But according to the Bureau of Justice Assistance Grants for Fiscal Year

2011, $35.6 million of the total $46.9 million of 2011 SCA grant funding was funneled to government agencies rather than community organizations that provide re-entry services for ex-offenders.

The State of North Carolina cut $4.78 million in funding for all of its prison work crews in 2009. It added back thirty-nine crews in 2010, but plans to continue adding work crews throughout 2011 disappeared when the thirty-nine crews added in 2010 were shut down for reasons cited as "budget reductions" by Keith Acree, then public affairs director of the state's Department of Public Safety. Details concerning the disappearing work crews have yet to be made public, so one can't help but wonder where this money is being funneled.

The three primary components of the criminal justice system lie and connive in order to look after each other and ensure that each of their images remain cloaked in perfection. This is evidenced by the provision of data by government agencies regarding other government agencies, and the unwarranted dismissals of inmate grievances and lawsuits; both of these cause penologists to misunderstand the sources of an abused inmate's debilitating emotional impairment and his inability to behave in a societally productive manner. This misunderstanding causes the inmate to be deemed incompetent and even injurious to any community in which he may reside, while prison administrators and the court system maintain their spotless records - at least in the eyes of penal system researchers. It's all one hell of a mess that needs to be addressed as soon as possible.

Regarding penologists, they seem to believe that the courts would not dismiss cases that are not worthy of dismissal. So when they comb through government statistics and see that almost all inmate lawsuits are dismissed by a court of law, they conclude that an overwhelming majority of inmate lawsuits ARE worthy of dismissal. Sometimes these experts go a little deeper and conclude that inmates just *feel* mistreated or unjustly wronged because they're not accustomed to dealing with authority figures and often misconstrue these authority figures' actions and intentions.

This is simply another misleading perception stemming from the practice of self-policing, from the fact that the agents of correction are NOT held accountable by anyone other than their criminal justice system cronies. This is just another inaccurate conclusion rooted in bias statistics, another misunderstood diagnosis that often results in prison staff becoming more brutal. The brutal prison staff members who are aware of penologists' work interpret the previously mentioned conclusion and the lack of resistance by penologists as proof that these experts are in agreement with such brutality. They believe that these scholars agree with prison officials' vicious quest to mistreat and "break" inmates. While executing such brutality, the prison staff encounters no opposition from penologists because the statistics, data, and information that these penologists used to analyze prison mechanisms is provided by the prison system itself. And, of course, the prison system will never grant these experts access to material that could potentially defile their image or provide penologists with a reason to oppose any prison practice, even though many of such reasons exist.

Simply put, penologists trust the penal system to be honest and to keep them in the light, but the penal system as well as its cronies (every other component of the criminal justice system) will lie and bury the truth in order to keep penologists in the dark. Both, this cronyistic belief in the justice system's integrity, along with the practice of self-policing deserves discrediting.

Government agencies, such as the NCDPS/DAC— Prisons, actively compile prison-related statistics that don't show the entire situation possibly because statistics of this nature would shine too bright of a light on the system's missteps. In addition, criminologists are alone when they try to conduct completely independent penal system statistical studies, and because this is an overwhelming task to tackle alone, they tend to rely heavily on the "fox's" statistical analysis of the "hen house" of which it's in charge. Most of these academics know that governments should not be trusted to provide meaningful and objective statistics that pertain to them and on which penological assessments will be based, but what choice do they have in a society that hates the people that criminologists study?

For those that have complete faith in government statisticians, note that governmental statistics did not highlight the failure of the Prison Society's "Pennsylvania System"— which classified and separated inmates according to their gender and the nature of their crimes. The data did not show the insanity and mental instability that resulted from this system's use of extreme isolation. Considering today's application of these same prehistoric Pennsylvania System methods, it's safe to assume one thing: change was inevitable, progress was not.

(I lean more towards statistical flaws than I do towards incompetence amongst academics because I truly believe in the mental wherewithal of most penologists and criminologists. Because of this belief, I simply cannot side with the argument that penal-system experts ignored statistics which accurately reflected the prison system's failures. This argument implies incompetence amongst penal-system researchers, an incompetence in which I disbelieve. In other words, the would-be statistical failure known as the "Pennsylvania System" is the system on which modern day North Carolina prisons are structured. If statistics do accurately document the system's failures and inadequacies, then the fact that North Carolina prisons are structured in this way reflects the incompetence of those responsible for the framework of this prison system. However, my argument is that they aren't incompetent; they just don't utilize reliable data sources.)

The Elmira System— introduced in New York in 1876— must have also been misrepresented by government statistical data. It failed because it judged detainees on their behavior as prisoners instead of on whether or not the inmates were ready for societal re-entry, and this is still the exact way in which North Carolina inmates are judged to this day. The logical consensus must be that this failed method of judgment was not reported as such to penological experts because if it were, it would have been addressed and eradicated from all modern penal systems. The same can be said about the poorly trained staffs, lack of funds, and ill-defined goals that plague prison reformative programs today in the same way that they plagued the rehabilitation programs of the 1930s.

Overlooking Festinger:

Many government-compiled statistics have buried failures such as these in the past, yet state officials continue to deem said statistics reliable. They do so even though they know concepts such as Leon Festinger's theory pertaining to cognitive dissonance cannot be statistically accounted for when analyzing the effectiveness of rehabilitation programs amongst prisoners. This theory is centered on the idea that people become uneasy when they encounter information that conflicts with their already established beliefs. It is supported by independent data that shows self-identified failures often avoid success even when it can be easily attained; this is because attainment of success would conflict with their beliefs in themselves as failures.

The reality of this theory is very acute in the lives of inmates. The ways in which this theory applies to self-identified criminals should not be overlooked. But when reviewing what government statistics purportedly identify as the most common reasons prisoners are not reformed, it is not only overlooked, it's trampled on. Self-identified criminals often avoid positive reformation because it conflicts with their belief in themselves as criminals, and rehabilitative measures continuously fail because statistics neither acknowledge nor address this conflict. (Even in the rare instances that penologists can analyze valuable social, cultural, economic and psychological factors such as Festinger's theory by reviewing statistics, their analyses are ignored when it comes to designing and actualizing the reformative programs that are based on these statistics.)

Extra-Penal Support:

Another major factor that is rarely statistically analyzed, a factor that is ignored and whose meaningfulness is consistently downplayed by statistical data, is "extra-penal support." This is defined as the reception of attention or affection by inmates from people that are not incarcerated. The importance of the provision of extra-penal support was acknowledged by former Virginia detainee R. Dwayne Betts in his memoir entitled *A Question of Freedom*. He wrote that "[b]eing in prison, I didn't expect to have the support of people I admired. And without that support I'm not sure what kind of rehabilitation can honestly take place."

He goes on further to say "I realized that there aren't many ways to thank people who help you from a distance...I'd gotten these letters and responded in kind, never really acknowledging that what was happening was a process of receiving love. There weren't many *good mornings* being passed around, there weren't many kind looks. So we all waited for the mail each afternoon and hoped to find a letter with a piece of the lives we couldn't touch there. In the letters, I found parts of my mom, my aunts and myself that I hadn't known existed. The worst part was that I found confirmation of my own absence...Our crimes took a machete to the bonds that made us family and left nothing but ink drying on paper to try to piece things back together."

The presence of extra-penal support determines whether or not an inmate is reformed moreso than any other factor, yet it seems not to have a place amongst statistical studies of inmate recidivism. This epitomizes absentmindedness. I've never met an inmate that avoided mental decrepitude without extra-penal support— which the inmate received as *love*. Some may view love as nothing more than a chemical reaction that causes delusion, but even the possessors of this perception cannot deny love's effects. (Those who are allergic to inmates, who believe that inmates are unlovable, and who are eager to vilify and oppress them upon their release because they haven't been sufficiently habilitated, need to realize that love is the key to this type of habilitation; plainly speaking, those with anti-inmate sentiments need to realize that people are sometimes the least lovable when they need love the most).

When love comes to a prisoner in the form of support from individuals that are beyond prison's grasp, the likelihood of this prisoner being productively reformed increases exponentially. Whenever an inmate receives what he perceives as "love," regardless of how faint or intense it is, it reduces the ability of prison's negative vices to take root. A strong argument could be made that meaningful upliftment and overall individual progression cannot occur in the life of a detainee without extra-penal support.

Why aren't statistics pushing the "experts" towards creating initiatives that reflect this argument? Is the problem with the second-hand government statistics or is the culprit an ineffective process for transforming statistical data into fruitful prison programs?

Punitive Social Osmosis (Criminality Suffusion into Above-Average Inmates):

This question concerning statistical problems simply cannot be answered adequately. These is because penologists who seek to generate their own statistical data, or conduct their own surveys or observational studies, still are forced to observe, analyze, and gather information from "samples" designated by government agencies. Their only option is to allow a government agency to select the members of a sample that will be studied under the guise of representing the entire prison population.

These agencies don't plan carefully to choose samples that will generate the most useful information. They seem to embrace unproductiveness by choosing the path of least resistance, which entails choosing samples that exclusively represent relatively average and below average inmates. Reliance upon these designated samples— mere portions of the detainee population— is extremely misleading because it causes researchers to ignore an important segment of inmates, a segment vital to the study of inmate reform.

Penal-system data and information provided by the government is the source of the selection bias that plagues penological statistical studies and inferences that are based upon these studies. When inferences or "logical conclusions" are made, the results should reflect the uncertainty involved in making inferences about the larger population, which in this context includes the segment of inmates that could contribute most to penological research— above average inmates. But amongst penologists, this seems to be avoided, mostly due to the fact that they've been conditioned to believe in the legitimacy of their statistical data (which, as previously stated, is of governmental origins and doesn't even acknowledge the existence of the aforementioned contributive segment).

The statistical data— in reflecting average and below average inmates only — causes penologists and initiators of reformative programs to leave the most capable and mentally developed detainees to be negatively influenced by the less capable incarcerated masses. Picture a swarm of average and below average prisoners on whom rehabilitative measures are based, yet with whom rehabilitative measures are not, and will never be, succeeding. Alongside this picture, imagine above average prisoners being herded towards recidivism. These elite convicts are neglected by prison administrations and as a consequence they're surrounded by average and below average crime addicts with nothing to prevent them from becoming addicts themselves. This social structure pushes them towards crime, coercing them into thinking and behaving like their criminous counterparts. This is a prison "social osmosis" in which criminality (of which the prison culture is mostly composed) is seeping into the least criminous members of the incarcerated environment, members least likely to recidivate and most likely to habilitate. It's as if above-average detainees are swimming in a pool of crime-addicted scorpions— they're bound to get stung at some point.

Data gathered through controlled experiments is compromised for the same reasons. The provision of sloppily and neglectfully compiled information by government agencies compromises these controlled experiments just like it does every other experiment. The special conditions (used for comparative purposes) created by penologists, independent statisticians, and other researchers often don't effectively mimic useful scenarios pertinent to prison culture oriented environments because of shallow governmental statistics.

In controlled experiments, these experts use computer software to simulate random events for comparison to observed data. The observed data is flawed (see Chapter One) and the random events are birthed by a computer program that also fails to account for prison culture and above-average inmates. (The comparisons are most likely conducted according to a free culture's criteria; a free culture mindset SHOULD be what inmates strive for, but the reality is that they're not striving for it mainly because of the way that the prison system is designed. Most inmates believe that the prison culture mindset is of the utmost relevance. They fail to recognize that prison culture has absolutely no significance outside of prison and they're not being taught otherwise.)

The result of statistical software— and the rehabilitative efforts that this software inspires— being designed without consideration of neither prison culture mindsets nor above-average inmates is extreme administrative ineffectiveness. It also contributes to the harmful marginalization of these above-average inmates. Prisoners that are least likely to recidivate are being herded, once again, towards recidivism while programs and prison administrators continue to fail to habilitate the prisoners that are most likely to recidivate. This is all due to systemic disregard, misleading data, and academics' monocultural approach to studying inmate reform and rehabilitation.

Punitive Social Osmosis (Flaws in Data Processing):

As one can imagine, processing social, behavioral, academic, and psychological information in the form of data entries pertaining to tens of thousands of inmates can be exhausting. The dispersion of data (defined below), computed with all things considered, can be very significant.

Some penological statisticians go about developing and processing statistics by first identifying or defining the "average inmate" using sociocultural, personality, intelligence, psychological, and even economic factors and jargon. They then calculate the "distances" that individual inmates are above or below this average inmate. These distances are called the *dispersion*. When the dispersion is listed, inmates with equal distances are grouped together. This type of list is known as a *frequency distribution*.

If I were to calculate the average distance listed in this frequency distribution, this average would be what's referred to as the *standard deviation*. Multiplying this average distance from the average inmate (the standard deviation) times itself would produce what's known as the *variance*. Penological statisticians often encounter very high values for the variance and the standard deviation of inmate-related data, and these high values mean that the inmate-related data is very spread out.

With this being said, a drastic problem becomes obvious when frequency distributions and arithmetic averages are developed, analyzed, and relied upon when structuring reformative initiatives. The use of *mean* (the mathematical operation that's more commonly known as the "average") in computing a standard deviation is worthy of scrutiny here. In *Arithmetic for College Students, 6ᵗʰ Edition*, D. Franklin Wright wrote that "many people feel that the mean [average] is relied on too much in reporting central tendencies for data...because a few very high items can distort the picture that a mean paints of central tendency." This excerpt undoubtedly applies to the process of defining the "average inmate" as well as to other arithmetic averages prevalent throughout penelogical statistical measures.

I'll clarify this excerpt with one example. The intelligence quotients (IQs) of eight individuals are as follows: 75, 76, 81, 81, 85, 87,108 and 151. For this set of data the mean of 93 is much less representative of the overall picture, especially when compared to the median of 83. This is because the one high IQ of 151 raises the mean considerably.

If these were the IQs of eight detainees their intellectual capacity as a group would be slightly misrepresented by the mean of 93. If this mean was exclusively considered, one would almost refuse to believe that half of this sample of inmates is close to being declared mentally retarded. I wish to dissuade penelogical statisticians from applying averages alone in certain circumstances, because as you may now see, they tend to be misrepresentative.

Practically speaking, let's say that inmate classifications and the distribution of rehabilitative resources are done according to the "distances" that particular inmates are above or below the defined average. If inmate "A" and inmate "B" have the same incarceration date, the same charges, the same sentences, and if they are both ten units away from the average, they would be grouped together and given the same reformative treatment. However, this grouping method (the core of frequency distributions) doesn't take into account that inmate "A" chose to breeze through his IQ test, randomly selecting answers to about a third of the questions and giving very little thought to the rest. Also, inmate "A," after five years in prison, has never seen nor spoken to a psychologist, a psychiatrist, a psychoanalyst, a counselor, a behavior specialist, a therapist, nor any other type of social worker. His brief periodical meetings with his high-school educated case worker are of little importance (and by "brief" I mean that the case worker asks inmate "A" if he has any questions, inmate "A" says that he does not, then the case worker dismisses him— end of meeting). The system knows nothing about this inmate beyond the fact that he's remained relatively infraction-free and that he has completed two or three vocational courses. His behavioral tendencies, social flexibility, emotional intelligence, financial position, verbal skills, and overall societal compatibility never get analyzed or assessed. Nobody even knows that his recorded IQ of 83 is about thirty points lower than his actual IQ, and that his post-prison plans entail volunteering to help educate impoverished youth.

Because of this lack of knowledge, inmate "A" will be grouped together with inmate "B." They're about the same age, with the same number of vocational courses completed, very few disciplinary infractions as well as recorded IQ's of 83. They both will be exposed to the same type of reformative treatment due to their similarities on paper, so-to-speak. Yet inmate "B" really does have have an IQ of 83. He was also raised in a very broken home that never transcended poverty and he plans to go home as soon as possible so that he can brutally murder his children's mother and her new boyfriend. No logical person would group these two inmates together when determining their rehabilitative needs.

Inmate "A" is a well-spoken, well-read, well-behaved product of affluency that simply made a bad decision. Inmate "B" is inarticulate, averse to education and mental enhancement, rude, and in agreement with those that promote criminality. He also believes that he's in prison *not* because of poor decision-making on his behalf but because of societal conditions beyond his control. No knowledgeable and competent individual would classify these detainees identically unless their motives were impure, neglectful, and/or malicious.

In prison, however, this type of classification, this sort of "grouping together" is protocol and its harmful effects are quite obvious to members of the prison culture. (The main effect being the reality that the inmate "B"s ALWAYS negatively influence the inmate "A"s due to the fact that there are really fifty different versions and varying degrees of inmate "B" embodied in fifty different inmates for every one embodiment of inmate "A".)

In spite of this, penological frequency distributions continue to group and classify inmate "A" together with inmate "B" when rehabilitation and potential recidivism are being studied. This is a mistake for a variety of reasons, a significant one being that regardless of how much work goes into defining the "average" inmate, absolutely no resources are dedicated to substantially analyzing the inmates that will be compared to this "average" inmate. No energy is expended towards really getting to know the inmate "A"s and the inmate "B"s. I, throughout many years of detainment thus far, have never conversed with— let alone been personally reviewed by— anyone other than my fellow prisoners. (Shallow meetings with a case worker do not register on the scale of significance.)

Nobody, other than my intellectual colleague, J. Vincent Hurley, and a few faithful correspondents, knows anything about my personality, my social flexibility (or lack thereof), my intellectual capabilities, my post-prison plans, or whether or not my season of confinement has enhanced or butchered my psyche. These factors are important when determining whether or not someone has been reformed, whether or not an inmate is prepared to be released, and whether or not an inmate has been productively punished. But surprisingly, they play no role in the development of frequency distributions— from which standard deviations are calculated. This means that on paper and in penology classrooms the figurative inmate "A" will perpetually be indecipherable from inmate "B."

Throughout his confinement inmate "A" will be pushed into programs and classes designed for inmates with double digit intelligence quotients barely beyond mentally retarded levels— classes that will fail to challenge, educate, or encourage him, classes with which he'll become frustrated. This frustration will only intensify the misery that comes along with being incarcerated. After a while, he'll become acutely aware of his misery, and this awareness will make him wonder why the system is punishing him so intensely, more so than his less competent peers.

Inmate "A" will wonder why administrators feel the need to inflict psychological harm upon him instead of recognizing that simply being in prison itself is his punishment, and a sufficient one to say the least. If he neither hides nor suppresses his relative intelligence, he'll also be demonized, ostracized, and verbally attacked by his mentally inferior peers for reasons that are beyond the scope of these writings. Eventually this will cause inmate "A" to become bitter and develop, at the very least, deep disdain for other members of the prison culture as well as what they identify as the criminal justice system (this disdain frequently grows to include all societal elites, be they judicial, corporate, political, social, etc).

Needless to say, his post-prison plans will eventually go downhill. They will start out being noble, then they'll drop down to selfish; from selfish they'll become unproductive, then harmful, and finally diabolical. The intensity of this regression depends on how long his incarceration lasts— osmosis depends on duration. While inmate "A"s life is heading downward, spiraling toward entropy, inmate "B" will continue to live on as a non-reformed criminous ignoramus on whom rehabilitation initiatives did not, and will never, work. To further highlight this moral and societal injustice I must note that inmate "A," a humanitarian with an IQ in excess of 113, and inmate "B", a career criminal with an IQ of 83, will be released at the same time regardless of how majestic or heinous their post-prison plans may be.

Nonexistent Progress Reports and Prison's Purpose: I fear that the

current ways in which statistical methods and measures are applied to North Carolina penal research may do more harm than good. This is because there are no mechanisms in place that accurately measure prisoners' mental and behavioral conditions within the North Carolina Department of Public Safety/Division of Adult Correction— Prisons. This is really crazy, don't you think?

If rehabilitation is the goal, why is it never measured? Do the experts even know how to measure rehabilitation? Are there no statistics that indicate the "average" inmate's level of rehabilitation after various durations of confinement— after one year, after three years, after ten years? Considering that the existence of these statistics is highly questionable, how do penologists or other agents of criminal justice determine whether or not rehabilitation is occurring with an individual detainee, especially in the absence of behavioral, psychological, and mental examination?

In the state of North Carolina, the punitive system has no evaluation arrangement in place to determine when an inmate has been adequately reformed. This is quite unfortunate because my experience has made the effects of such an "evaluationless" arrangement very sharp. Consider that immediately after a prisoner's habilitation level peaks, as soon as it reaches its highest crest, it begins to descend towards a trough of blinding bitterness and hatred if the inmate remains confined. But again, there's nothing in place to monitor this social, emotional, and mental fluctuation between reform and destructive hatred.

Furthermore, this bitterness and hatred is very abstract and free-floating; it has no target and no object.

75

It tends to manifest unproductively as a dislike for people that are not similar to the subject (this includes a devaluation of women), an even more piercing distaste for authority figures, an inability to withstand criticism, an irrational eagerness to take an aggressively defensive stance even when not being attacked, and sometimes it even comes out as a zest for behaving even more unlawfully. This "learning-of-one's-lesson-only-to-descend-towards-hatred" concept is a reality that hinders habilitation, yet it also fails to be statistically documented and studied.

This statistical malfeasance only seems sensible to those who believe that incarceration is for punishment alone, rather than rehabilitation through perceived punishment. The penologists that hold such a belief should know that it is in direct opposition to the position of Cesare Beccaria— who is widely regarded as the father of modern criminology. In his 1764 book, *On Crimes and Punishments,* Beccaria rightly argued that the only purpose of punishment should be to prevent future misconduct. This is one tenet of the classical school with which penologists should be aligned. For those who are not aligned with this classic tenet, for those who still maintain that the goal of incarceration is to punish for punishment's sake, I would like to pose a question— how does anyone know when a prisoner has been sufficiently punished if punishment levels are also never measured?

I would like to also ask why there are no statistics that indicate the amount of time that it takes to effectively punish the "average" prisoner. Penologists don't know the answer to this latter question, yet it is blatantly obvious to the above-average members of the prison culture. These members also know a little secret that I would like to share with you. This secret is that the calculation and formulation of these punish-the-average-prisoner statistics is impossible due to the fact that most inmates don't even view their stint of confinement as "punishment" in the conventional sense. They tend to view it as either a common, if not natural, progression or occurrence for people "like them," or as an unwarranted attack on their very personhood. Knowing this, one cannot avoid asking the question: how can it be punishment if the person being punished doesn't view it as such?

In addition to this, psychologists will readily admit that different people may have different interpretations of the same experience. Revocation of a child's television privileges may be equivalent to a stern warning for one child, while another child may equate it with corporeal punishment. Likewise, the prison experience may be viewed as a vacation or a "break" by a crack addict, as a slap on the wrist by a drug dealer, or as a death sentence by a politician, even though the experience itself remains constant.

Because of this proven principle and for punishment to be most effective, most can agree that it should be tailored to fit the individual and the situation. To not ensure that the punishment fits the person and the offense is to administer abortive punishment and uncertain discipline. One wouldn't stone a child for missing one homework assignment, nor merely withhold one week's allowance from a child that got caught with a gun in school. To do so would be a counterproductive misappropriation of punishment.

In reality, decent parents neither punish nor discipline their children without considering the children's ages, genders, intelligence, personalities, characters, and past actions. This is to ensure that the punishment is effective. This is to guarantee that harmful abuse and fruitless leniency are both avoided, and that discipline is certain.

All of these considerations determine what type of punishment will be the most useful, yet the authors of the North Carolina penal system continue to adhere to a "one-type-fits-all" method of criminal justice (prison) and a cookie-cutter method of administering that justice (structured sentencing).

Even those who believe that incarceration's purpose is to maintain a sense of justice in society seem aloof when they ignore the harm that's caused by "one-type-fits-all" punishments. As unreliable as statistics can be, none (nor any other type of evidence) support the idea that structured sentencing— or prison in general— either reduces the crime rate or enhances a so-called sense of justice by incapacitating offenders or by discouraging others from breaking the law. (The streets create new criminals all the time, and neither new nor old criminals think about prison time before they commit crimes.)

But in spite of this lack of statistical support, some people continue to assert that crime is the result of disregard for rules and laws, a lack of respect for authority (i.e. agents of law enforcement and criminal justice), and an overall weakened sense of societal justice. They proclaim that the former disregard and lack of respect are responsible for the latter weakened reverence for societal justice. Therefore— as the rhetoric goes— eradication of these two perceived "character flaws" would promote a sense of justice thereby reducing the crime rate. Possessors of this belief advocate prison systems that are designed to instill reverential respect (indistinguishable from fear) of authority figures into prisoners.

This advocacy is producing rotten fruit. North Carolina prisons are effectively training inmates to "fear" authority officials in the same way that civilians "feared" dictators throughout the Libyan, Tunisian, Egyptian, and Syrian revolts (the Arab Spring) in recent years. But just like the Arab Spring, this fear isn't manifesting amongst inmates as reverence, as these advocates claimed it would. They fail to take into consideration that people tend to hate what they fear, a notion that anyone that's even remotely aware of prison social mechanisms would immediately recognize amongst detainees.

This fear of authority figures is manifesting as an intense hatred of authority figures, a hatred that the previously mentioned advocates themselves identify as the cause of crime. This means that the prison system is intensifying crime-producing character flaws within its

78

inhabitants just before releasing these inhabitants into society, where, in the event of future crime commission, they'll be vilified for not "learning their lesson" in prison! (Simply put, a hatred of authority causes crime, so let's fight crime by making people hate authority even more...this is silly shit at its finest!)

In a 1973 publication entitled the *Task Force Report on Corrections,* the National Advisory Commission on Criminal Justice Standards and Goals issued a recommendation that "...no new institutions for adults should be built and existing institutions for juveniles should be closed." They found that "the prison, the reformatory, and the jail have achieved only a shocking record of failure. There is overwhelming evidence that these institutions create crime rather than prevent it."

This coincides with what Michelle Alexander noted when she wrote that "[a]s recently as the mid-1970s, the most well respected criminologists were predicting that the prison system would soon fade away...[T]he notion that our society would be much better off without prisons— and that the end of prisons was more or less inevitable— not only dominated mainstream academic discourse in the field of criminology but also inspired a national campaign by reformers demanding a moratorium on prison construction."

During these times "fewer than 350,000 people were being held in prisons and jails nationwide, compared with more than two million people today. The rate of incarceration in 1972 was at a level so low that it no longer seems in the realm of possibility, but for moratorium supporters, that magnitude of imprisonment was egregiously high."

I can't help but wonder what these supporters think now. Why hasn't the intensity of their fervor increased in excess of 570 percent in the same way that the prison population has? Does this explain the relatively high recidivism rates? And is this not being acknowledged because reading and interpreting penological statistics has led people to believe that measuring psychological differences, mental capacities, and rehabilitative effectiveness is useless? Is penology leading people to believe that the current standard operating procedure will suffice even though very much measurable regression and devolution has occurred? Maybe this blatant ineffectiveness is not ineffectiveness at all, which would be the case if the criminal justice system's goal is neither rehabilitation nor punishment, but to make victims of crime feel a little bit better. (Such "emotional massages" accomplish nothing as far as reducing crime is concerned, but they do encourage people to refrain from looking too sharply or critically at the criminal justice system.)

Regardless of one's position on this, or how one chooses to answer the previously asked questions, what is certain is that the people that run the prison system are either misleading the societal masses or consistently falling short of their goals. Sophisticated intellectuals and autodidacts in my situation— Incarcerated Thinkers— can easily see that the concept of prison preserving a sense of societal justice is a complete falsehood that's inconsistent with any measure of sensibility. In reality, this society's justice system only seeks to maintain a sense of "justice" amongst those that are NOT at the top of the societal hierarchy. Duke University anthropologist William O'Barr wrote in the Duke Law Journal that "...lower social-status witnesses, by virtue of the way they speak, may have less credibility and thus a lesser chance of a fair hearing than higher-status witnesses. This, of course, is not congruent with the ideals of American justice." (A great deal has been written about the ways in which one's status, financial backing, and influential social connections alter the outcome of what are supposed to be objective investigations and court proceedings, so I won't go into too much detail about it here.)

My argument is clear (and VERY open for a debate if you're interested). Reflective and objectively conducted statistical studies are a rarity; and even if they weren't, they still would neither undergird nor validate any of the stated and widely accepted purposes of imprisonment. Any statistics that support the idea that prison rehabilitates, reforms, or punishes criminals, or promotes a sense of justice in society, are inaccurate and do not deserve to be taken seriously.

Responses to Statistical Analyses and Histograms:

I am not alone in believing that the ineffectiveness that stems from the previously opined upon aspects of statistical research is much more complex than a couple of intentional or accidental statistical errors or miscues. Even if penologists were aided with unbiased statistics compiled by independent entities, my research (which is admittedly limited) still leads me to believe that we all need to help penologists respond to statistical data more effectively. Currently, prison officials and legislators taunt these responses by failing to aid in the accomplishment of any of penologists' stated goals, more specifically the goals that pertain to ensuring public safety by habilitating convicts.

If I were to gather and display data that lists the number of inmates at various levels of being scholastically and morally educated, reformed, and habilitated, I would probably use a histogram to do so (or a simple bar or line graph). This histogram would have population counts ascending vertically on the y-axis and ascending numerical measurements of inmates' readiness-for-release levels on the x-axis. (A wide variety of social, behavioral, mental, psychological, intellectual, familial, economic, and personality-related factors would be considered when determining the ways in which "readiness-for-release" levels may be numerically measured.) The data displayed on this histogram would, as previously stated, coincide with the central limit theorem. In other words, it would be shaped like a bell.

Credible and influential inmate reformists concerned with societal improvement would respond to my histogram by expending their energy on programs that target the inmates occupying the lower LEFT region of the aforementioned "bell" (this region of the histogram is where inmates with the lowest readiness-for-release levels would be located). Precisely this "targeting" is the reason that reformative efforts invariably fail...end of story.

To allow inmates with relatively average or below average readiness-for-release levels to be the focal point around which all rehabilitative efforts revolve is to imply that the goal of penologists, prison officials, and legislators is NOT to improve society by reducing the crime/recidivism rate. Instead, it leads me to believe that the system's single overarching goal is to produce "conformed inmates," to even out the average inmate caliber by neglecting and therefore reducing the readiness-for-release levels of inmates in the lower RIGHT region of the previously mentioned histogram (this region being occupied by inmates with the highest readiness-for-release levels). In short, such a focal point supports the idea that prison's goal is to appear to be trying to make the "worst" inmates better. This is only an appearance, a façade, so of course they fail to accomplish this fake goal; but there's also some collateral damage. This damage consists of making the "best" individuals worse.

This concept of devoting massive amounts of energy and resources towards the upliftment of the least capable inmates (a devotion that, historically, has languished) while neglecting the most capable inmates is much more harmful in actuality than I'm capable of conveying literarily. Realistically speaking, it's a concept that promotes population-wide mental equalization by attempting, but miserably failing, to raise up the "lower level" inmates while very effectively bringing down the "higher level" inmates. It's nothing less than extreme institutional, intellectual communism.

CHAPTER 4:
A Complement to Statistical Analyses and Perceptions

"So we face a choice: will we take individuals whom we have judged unfit for life in the free world, expose them to further violence, destabilize them psychologically and deny them serious treatment for addiction, trauma, and mental illness? Or will we attempt to create a system of support and rehabilitation for the incarcerated? For their sake, and our own, the answer seems clear."

—James Forman Jr
Yale Law School Professor of Law

"Racial Critiques of Mass Incarceration: Beyond the New Jim Crow"
Published in Prison Legal News July 2012, Vol. 23 No. 7

It's difficult to identify an area in which "average-ism" (intense focus on the average while neglecting the above-average) is more widespread than it is amongst inmate reformists— a category which includes many penologists. In few other industries, fields, or sectors are the "normal" or the "less than normal" subjects the highlighted center of attention when it comes to upliftment, advancement, or progression of any kind.

The best high school students (scholastically speaking) are the ones that get the scholarships; the most productive workers are the ones that get the promotions when all else is equal; the best strippers get the most tips; the most capable athletes get the best and most extensive training to become even better at their sport; only the highest performing military persons advance swiftly through the ranks— again with all else being equal. Even in major political campaigns, the normal party members are secondary to the relatively few non-partisans, or "independents," who seem to get the most attention and who often determine the outcome of political elections.

In each of these examples (the latter being a possible exception due to cronyistic political practices and oligarchic imperialism...that was very "radical left-wingish" of me, wasn't it?), highlighting the elites that are undeniably worthy of their elite status gives the remaining subjects something to strive for. It gives them a pattern on which the design of their lives can be based, or a proven blueprint for success, if you will. Focusing on the "best" performers— those who most resemble the ideal— nurtures an environment of "reaching forward," of pursuing betterment, and of fruitful competition. Although this right-winged concept of catering to the elites consistently fails when applied to economic issues and arenas, applying it in purely social situations that are immune to greed and exploitation often produces valuable fruit. In other words, education, instruction, mental upliftment, and intellectual and moral progression are arguably the only instances where the conservative "trickle-down theory" has been proven to be helpful for *all* involved parties.

Penologists that favor inmate reform aim to refine and enhance the intellects and moral compasses of the incarcerated. They seek to educate, enlighten, and mentally uplift prisoners. This can only be actualized if the penal system sets its sights on the upliftment of the most capable detainees, if it applies this trickle-down theory to all of its rehabilitative programs. The effects of structuring the penal system in a way that cultivates the intellectual growth of above-average inmates are two-fold.

First, these more advanced inmates would be able (and willing) to contribute SUCCESSFULLY to the growth and development of their less capable counterparts. (If their efforts were to combine with those of penologists, inmate rehabilitation advocates, educators, and other prison reformists, this contribution would be much more significant.) These above-average inmates fully understand prison culture and have a much stronger motivation to aid in the overall evolution of their fellow prisoners— if my fellow prisoners were smarter and more mature, then I wouldn't have to put up with so much silly crap every day. Lower caliber inmates are also more inclined to receive instruction from capable and articulate individuals with whom they can relate. This notion of "relatability" coincides with the second effect of redirecting the penal system's focus.

This second effect is the prison-culture-wide reality that average and below-average inmates will remain true to their very primitive tendency to "fit in." Conforming to their environment before passionately exterminating everything that could possibly cause them to be misaligned with said environment will always be their top priority. In response to re-structuring prison according to the needs of above-average convicts, the average and below-average convicts would pursue personal improvement because that is what their social environment would center around.

With individual development as the framework of prison, less evolved inmates would fulfill their desire to "fit in" by conforming to the intellectually progressive norm (which I'm arguing should replace what is currently prison's crime-friendly norm). As of right now, unintelligent, morally bankrupt, lawlessly savage, ambitionless inmates are in an inertia-like state. They are not overcoming this inertia; they consistently fail to transcend prison's pro-crime status quo because nothing is encouraging, let alone forcing, them to change directions.

Frederick Douglass once wrote that "if nothing is expected of a people, that people will find it difficult to contradict that expectation." This has never been more applicable to anyone than it is to today's incarcerated souls. Absolutely nothing in prison is requiring, expecting, nor persuading them to be anything more than what they are— criminals. These people have no immediate reasons to become better individuals, and they aren't foresightful enough to see the future benefits of self-improvement (a lack of foresight that is fostered, if not created, in the "pre-trial detainee" stage of one's induction into prison culture).

Having no drive to become a better person is a problem that can be solved by redesigning rehabilitation programs; turning a punitive establishment into a well-spring of intellectual activity would give less developed inmates an immediate reason to better themselves. As they develop mentally, they will become more foresightful.

Something must be done in order for progress to be made; a system-wide change is needed. If the system cannot require mental development from inmates, it should at least stop discouraging it and refrain from nourishing criminality.

Don't you agree with me? If not, you will when one of these jackasses gets out and breaks into your home while you're sleeping. Then you'll be screaming PRISON NEEDS TO STOP PROMOTING CRIME!!!

A major part of this crime promotion pertains to something that I cover in Part Two of this book—education programs behind bars. Throughout my season of incarceration thus far, I've been a student, a tutor, an informal instructor, a teacher's assistant, a proctor, and even a janitor responsible for cleaning the education department. I've had extensive involvement with all levels of prison education and classroom activity, and one crime-promoting factor seems to stand out right now: I have NEVER met a prisoner who failed a class for academic reasons. Hell, I've never even encountered *another* prisoner that knew or ever *heard of* someone failing a class for academic reasons.

I've seen inmates sleep for over an hour during class on a daily basis, hurl non-stop insults at the instructor, and be completely oblivious of the subject matter, and still receive passing grades for the course. This isn't a testament of the scholastic prowess of the incarcerated; this is confirmation that very little is expected let alone required from inmates, even in the one place where "try your best" is supposed to be somewhat of a mantra— school. It seems like every nook and cranny of prison confirms the old saying "from whom little is required little is given." (Inmates are the ones that suffer most when they "give little," so systemic reform is needed to prevent this modern day, thinly veiled self- genocide.)

In addition to such despicably low expectations, data collection methods, statistical applications, and inferences based on statistical data must stop leading experts down an avenue that focuses entirely on unresponsive, ambitionless, and comfortably unenlightened prisoners ("comfortably unenlightened" is such a great phrase; it's a perfect way to describe the guys in here).

For example, Stanford University psychologist Hazel Markus has written extensively about the mindsets of socioeconomic classes. She and her colleagues have found, broadly speaking, that the affluent value individuality, uniqueness, differentiation and personal achievement. They also discovered that people lower down on the socioeconomic ladder, which is where the previously referred to unresponsive inmates are located, tend to stress homogeneity, harmonious interpersonal relationships, and group affiliation.

There are some inmates that are "affluent-minded," meaning they share the same values that Markus attributed to upper-class people. They cherish the fact that they're not like the other inmates (uniqueness); they're eager to set themselves apart from prison's crime-loving herd (differentiation); and they're willing to set goals and to work hard to accomplish these goals (personal achievement). These affluent-minded inmates are the least likely to come back to prison when they are released, primarily because they possess what Markus identified as the rich-person value system.

Oftentimes though, instead of receiving proper attention, this fact is neglected. Instead of being recognized as one of the roots of habilitation, this value system is disregarded and pushed aside. This happens because of government-compiled statistics and a lack of respect for the field of penology.

When these statistics are given to penologists (penological statisticians, to be specific) these experts must analyze them by using what's been known as the *confirmatory method*– a technique used to distinguish between important differences in data and meaningless variations. These penologists basically have to sift through all of the data and determine what's useful and what can be overlooked. This process is very hard, tedious, time-consuming, and exhausting. Penologists must do it all by themselves before anything can be studied and examined. They're presented with a boatload of useless and mostly falsified numbers, and nobody respects their craft enough to step up and help them sort through it and identify what's vital and what's not. Because of this arrangement, penologists tend to disregard important information. More specifically, they often classify the values of the affluent inmates as meaningless.

This structure and other basic operating procedures along with ignorance of prison mechanisms and unnecessarily limited statistical studies, must be addressed and corrected before substantive improvement, widespread inmate reform, and overall advancement can materialize behind prison walls.

CHAPTER 5:
Flaws in Penological Case Studies

"[T]he slave went free; stood a brief moment in the sun; then moved back again toward slavery."

—*W.E.B. DuBois*
"Black Reconstruction in America"

A case study is defined as "an intensive analysis of an individual unit (as a person or community) stressing developmental factors in relation to environment." In a penological case study, a prison inmate is the individual unit, and his personality traits— psychological and behavioral— and the effects of certain social conditions are what gets analyzed. Elements such as his family history, environment, physical condition, education level, mental state, and social affiliations are all factored into the conduction of such penological case studies. The individual case histories produced by these studies are used to create or work out theories concerning the development of recidivistic tendencies, individual rejection of reformative initiatives, or other displays of criminous behaviors amongst current and former prisoners.

As you can see by this explanation, the structures of both case studies and case histories are not one-size-fits-all. They are tailored to fit the individual subject according to the previously referred to elements. Because these studies are so customized, the methods that guide them are very broad and subjective. This means that different techniques and approaches must frequently be applied to different subjects, even when they're selected from the same population and are very similar in all commonly recognizable ways.

I believe that penologists, as well as other researchers, understand the benefits of modularity.

However, I also believe they should recognize its shortcomings when it comes to doing case studies. Bluntly speaking, these academics should not use a universally applied model as a guide. The aforementioned subjectivity along with the maintenance of personal preferences pertaining to the logistics of case studies would really crack the foundation of such a model and jeopardize its reliability. My position here is undeniable and understandable, and it should be embraced. Different penologists conduct case studies in different ways. The format of these case studies depends on the individual inmate's condition. In keeping with my writings thus far, I must also admit that for me to criticize the *specific* use of these studies as a means of data collection is to somewhat delegitimize my position on this issue. To stay "legit," I must warn you that there are some major restrictions imposed upon my intellectual vision.

As things currently stand, my scope is very limited because of these restrictions (the two biggest "restrictions" are the crappy prison library and my lack of computer— let alone internet— access). Basically, if this chapter of my book were a person, he or she would be shackled. The lack of complete uniformity amongst researchers coupled with the need to customize penological case studies and my limited access to resources that expound on these case studies, all serve as intellectual manacles. At the risk of diluting my opinions, I must let you know beforehand that these manacles have left me with just one option: to opine on, and theorize about this subtopic in a very general manner.

William and Paul: Fifteen-year-old

William and his friend Paul were above average youths with precocious intellects. They were creative geniuses who were irrefutably unmatched by their peers and capable of life altering innovations. Both of them had not only solid values and impressive vision, but also the specific analytical tools necessary to make the components of their visions come to life.

As very young adults, they used these tools to start a software company— tools such as access to vital information, a supportive family, positive guidance, fiscally responsible guardians, educational resources, etc. (Many of these tools were enhanced when people began to recognize that William and Paul were intellectually poised to reach unimaginable societal heights.) Their eventual rise to the top of the computer software industry is unparalleled, even to this day. Their ascent is often regarded as the epitome of success obtained through the theoretical American experience, which includes hard work, mental adeptness, and the availability of progressive opportunities.

William "Bill" Gates and Paul Allen, the founders of Microsoft Corporation, are technological pioneers who excelled with impressive tenacity. They made a conscious decision to take advantage of the opportunities provided by their environment. As a result, they cultivated and nourished creative and critical thinking, as well as intellectual advancement and transcendence of the technological status quo. (Or, as we Incarcerated Thinkers like to say, they did their damn thang!)

But what if things had transpired a little differently for these two? What if their lives had been flooded by negative social and intellectual tidal waves and other hindrances to personal development? What if their friends and families, their schools, and their teachers had interacted with them as if their needs were equivalent to the needs of their less intelligent peers? What if every single book, essay, industry journal, scholastic program, as well as every available media source to which they were exposed was designed and constructed according to the intellects of their less capable, less ambitious, and less creative counterparts? What if they weren't allowed to surround themselves with people that challenged their minds nor were able to partake in productive dialogical exchanges of any kind?

Imagine Gates and Allen being reared in such environments, full of proud ignoramuses that treat mental upliftment like malaria. Now imagine a seemingly omnipresent "Being" randomly selecting an individual from Gates' and Allen's childhood surroundings (one of those proud anti-malaria ignoramuses). Now picture this "Being" designing Gates' and Allen's entire— now inescapable— environment based on the needs of this one ignoramus.

If this scenario were true, one can only guess what Gates' and Allen's societal status would have turned out to be. I think that it's safe to assume that their plights would've been tougher and their ascensions would have been a bit more complicated. It's also reasonable to say that if this scenario would've transpired, the very frameworks of both Microsoft Corporation and the Bill and Melinda Gates Foundation would exist in a different form than they do today, if they even existed at all. This would obviously be a moral injustice; this would be a stain on America's reputation as "the land of opportunity." To have blocked Gates' and Allen's pursuit of technological evolution, paradigmatic enhancement, and the promotion of humanitarianism would have been unforgivably sacrilegious not only to these intellectual gladiators but to this nation's ideals as a whole.

Yet "blockage" of this nature is occurring daily here in North Carolina amongst thousands of confined souls. It's promoted and held up as a staple of social "control" behind prison walls and behind the closed office doors of prison administrators. The Incarcerated Thinkers are the Williams and Pauls; the autocratic prison system is the omnipresent Being; and average and below-average inmates are definitely proud ignoramuses.

The omnipresent prison system (i.e. legislators, prison officials, and researchers) often selects random inmates for assessment and analysis. The results of these assessments are used to construct and design inmate habilitative programs, as well as to determine the availability of certain literary resources in certain

92

situations. Keep in mind that habilitative programs and literary resources are inmates' ONLY means of mental development and social progression. This "Being's" random selection of an individual subject is the first step in conducting a case study.

Researchers tend to rely on such random selections because in theory, randomness eliminates prejudices from the selection process. They also tend to believe that selecting an inmate at random will most enable them to objectively identify the "average inmate," whom they will use to pinpoint the needs of the entire prison population. Once this is done, they usually begin defining ways in which to address these needs and improve this "average." Therefore, having an average inmate available for analysis is vital for the genesis and the progression of their case study.

This is flawed for a number of reasons, the most significant being the fact that researchers appear to be oblivious of how truly *hopeless* the average inmate is.

Mental, Environmental, And Parental Deficiencies: In a little over six

years thus far, I've been housed at five different institutions across the state of North Carolina. From Elizabeth City, where one inhales the salty air that drifts in from the not-too-distant oceanfront, to looking through a cell window in Morganton, unable to see the top of the massive rock formation that is protruding from the foot of the Blue Ridge Mountains. I've had hundreds of raw, in-depth, and untainted interactions with countless prisoners of different creeds, races, and ages. No known criminologist, penologist, inmate reformist, nor penal system researcher even claims to have had such extensive and intensive dealings and encounters with inmates in such a relatively short period of time.

My unfortunate experiences as a detainee have left me with a very unconventional perspective. This perspective is what makes me uniquely qualified to elaborate on the condition of the average inmate. I have no hidden agenda; I'm willing to criticize and be criticized; and if the idea of political correctness was a human, I would tell him to kiss my ass (unless political correctness was a woman— then I probably would just flirt with her). My current societal positioning— incarceration— along with my interest in the Life of the Mind serves as validation of my qualification to describe the plight of the average inmate before, during, and after imprisonment.

My assertion that this average inmate is "hopeless" is deeply rooted in observatory and empirical data and information. As many people should know, this individual did not grow up in an affluent environment. His childhood surroundings were not overly populated with opportunities to progress and succeed in society. What few opportunities that did exist in his environment were not advertised amongst the youth.

As a consequence of such a sad arrangement, this average inmate was reared in a poverty-stricken and crime-infested community, and he was completely unaware of how to escape. He didn't receive basic parental teachings— personal accountability, a sense of autonomous individuality, an appreciation of education, and so forth. His parents didn't even provide sufficient motor stimulation for him so that as an infant he could develop more neurons and nerve pathways which could've enhanced his intelligence and his learning capabilities. (Without sufficient motor stimulation his unused neurons simply atrophied and vanished.)

An extreme lack of money only further complicated things. As Lisa Miller wrote in "The Money-Empathy Gap," which was published in *New York* magazine, "Public-health research has long shown that poverty can have devastating effects on the brain. At three-years-old, poor kids have vocabularies that are three times smaller than their better off peers...In poor children, executive function is not as developed as it is in more affluent children, which means they have a harder time sorting and organizing information, planning ahead, and coping in the event of changed circumstances."

With this being said, it can easily be seen that from the very beginning, the average inmate is affected by the same impairments as people with mental retardation: intellectual underdevelopment, an inability to adjust (without drastic measures) to socially or culturally different environments, no capacity for meaningful personal relationships, nor for dealing with problems of attention deficit (hyperactive) disorder.

Harmful Self-Fulfilling

Stigmas: The upbringing of the average inmate is

not alone in contributing to his hopelessness. It's true he is an impoverished, mentally and socially underdeveloped, uneducated product of less than ideal parenting that is unaware of any path of upward mobility, and surrounded by crime and drugs. It's also true that he has been in this very sad condition almost since birth. However, in addition to these things, he has spent his life being maligned by influential social simpletons who were unaware of his rugged plight. They labeled him in a way that merely erected another obstacle that he will likely fail to overcome. This individual was reared in a harmful environment, denied guidance, and was categorized as a delinquent. To cope with these things (especially the hopelessly negative stigma and societal marginalization) he simply embraced what was readily available— criminality

As Michelle Alexander acknowledged in the following excerpt, this coping mechanism is what fuels both damaging stigmas and mass incarceration: "There is absolutely nothing abnormal or surprising about a severely stigmatized group embracing their stigma. Psychologists have long observed that when people feel hopelessly stigmatized, a powerful coping strategy— often the only apparent route to self-esteem— is embracing one's stigmatized identity. [This embracing act] is never merely a psychological maneuver; it is a political act, an act of resistance and defiance in a society that seeks to demean a group based on an inalterable trait [such as where one was raised]."

She goes on to say that "[o]nly by fully embracing the stigma itself can one neutralize the sting and make it laughable...Yet when these young people do what all severely stigmatized groups do— try to cope by turning to each other and embracing their stigma in a desperate effort to regain some measure of self-esteem— we, as a society, heap more shame and contempt upon them...When we are done shaming them, we throw up our hands and then turn our backs as they are carted off to jail." Although this applies universally to the average inmate (albeit in varying intensities) further analysis and classification of him can be made.

Openly Criminous and Delusional

: After basking in the criminal stigma, embracing criminality with their actions, and then getting locked up, most individuals lean towards one of two sides of a well-concealed dichotomy. I'm sharply aware of this hidden dichotomy (like a career politician is sharply aware of the political dichotomy— Republican and Democrat) because I've lived in prison for my entire adult life. As a result, I've learned that in excess of eighty-six percent of North Carolina detainees unknowingly put themselves into one of two categories: openly criminous or delusional.

The openly criminous individuals embrace criminality. They're unashamed, if not proud, of their unlawful past and they eagerly anticipate what they predict will be a criminous post-prison future. They shun and devalue education and enlightenment of any kind while simultaneously exalting and glorifying all forms of perceived entertainment and criminality (crimes involving the mistreatment of children are probably the only exceptions).

It isn't uncommon for openly criminous inmates to flock to the television in droves whenever a deprecatory rap star, a drug bust, or gun violence is on the screen. They spend the bulk of their prison time promoting, talking, and reading poorly written novels about selling drugs, gang membership, and the objectification/abuse of women; drug use is their primary route to pleasure; drug dealing is their desired career; illegal firearms are their accessory of choice. These self-professed criminals will be released from prison only to return quickly, get murdered, or live off of the resources of a gullible woman that's willing to satisfy and cater to their every need and be completely acquiescent to their every whim. (If you're a woman and you're reading this, please contact me so that I can tell you how to NOT become this "gullible woman".)

The delusional inmates, on the other hand, often trick people into believing that they are further away from being openly criminous than they actually are. They often claim to be done with the "crime life," professing that their children are their top priority or that they're just tired of being locked up and they've had enough of prison. These individuals routinely say that they would like to live a morally upstanding and societally legitimate life, and they can be quite convincing unless one seriously heeds what seems like mere Freudian slips and innuendoes. For example, every once in a while they'll say that they plan to search for employment upon their release. But with their next breath they'll say that they refuse to struggle or be poor for any length of time. The implication here is that income-generating criminality is still an option— a last option that they may claim to want to avoid, but still an option nonetheless.

Probe a little and ask these delusional inmates where their job search will occur, what marketable skills they possess, or what skills or interests need to be cultivated in order to expand their employment options, and watch the blank stares you'll get. Ask where they will reside until they find a job or how they'll use the Work Opportunity Tax Credit and federal bonding programs to their advantage and you'll receive silence as

97

a response. Ask how they'll utilize the Employment Security Commission and the Job Link Career Center, or what they plan to put on their resume and only one answer will be given: "I don't know."

It's blatantly obvious that they set themselves up for failure, and oftentimes upon failing, they fall back on their last option (i.e. a life of crime). They delude themselves by thinking that nothing more than a desire to avoid prison and a proclamation of this desire is needed to live an upstanding post-prison life and to avoid the lawless activities that their lives once revolved around. This delusion is so strong that these inmates, after being made aware of their intellectual folly, still refuse to expend energy on finding solutions to the previously mentioned rhetorical questions. Being aware of their own lack of preparation is barely a faint glimmer when compared to the blindingly bright light that is their allegiance to, and belief in, this delusion.

Both the openly criminous prisoner and his delusional counterpart, upon their release, will be like the liberated slave that turns back toward slavery after briefly glimpsing the sun. In other words, they will leave prison and come right back. This dichotomy is basically universal amongst this state's captives, so don't think that it'll be easy to locate an inmate that it doesn't apply to. The selection of a prison inhabitant at random will yield an average inmate who is destined for criminality and who refuses to do what is necessary to transcend this self-imposed destiny— regardless of which end of the penal dichotomy he leans towards.

This destiny is constantly re-fulfilled over and over again. It continuously plays out in the lives of average inmates on both sides of the penal dichotomy. As historical and modern day recidivism rates can attest, selecting a random detainee with the hope of designing reformative initiatives and rehabilitative programs according to the needs of this "average" inmate is quite a fruitless endeavor. This is because a random selection will probably yield someone who is openly criminous or delusional. Aiming these programs towards uplifting these two types of people, people who aren't willing to allow themselves to be uplifted and who are persistently encouraged to despise refinement, will consistently result in missed targets. Selecting and relying upon the average convict as a source of information is completely futile and unavailing because he will forever turn back toward slavery after briefly glimpsing the glow of freedom— especially if "slavery" (prison) continues to consist of rampant crime promotion. Trust me on this!

Wasted Human Resources: The

collateral damage that is produced by designing programs according to the needs of average inmates (whether they're openly criminous or delusional) is just as tragic as the fact that these programs continue to fail to habilitate these average inmates. Oppression of the exceptional inmates, the Incarcerated Thinkers, is the collateral damage that I'm referring to. These exceptional inmates desire personal evolution and societal improvement. However, they spend their entire sentences being bombarded with classes, teachers, and programs designed for, and oriented towards, the "average" (i.e. self-deprecating and subtly self-genocidal) inmate.

Incarcerated versions of Bill Gates and Paul Allen, in light of these poorly structured programs, cannot immerse themselves in environments that cultivate and nourish creative and critical thinking, intellectual advancement, and transcendence of what, in prison, is the crime-friendly status quo. Outsiders may believe that enrollment in programs such as "C.B.I.," "Thinking for a Change," "Human Resources Development," and "Cognitive Learning" sounds enticing. They may even believe that these programs are the first step in creating a productive prison environment. But what these outsiders don't know is that the only growth that occurs in these classes is criminogenic in nature. The only thing that inmates in these classes learn is that the prison programs that aim to address mental and social deficiencies are really shams that accomplish little

99

beyond making the system look like it's TRYING to reform inmates.

These classes produce nothing meaningful because of the administration's avid, yet baseless, belief that reform should begin with the average—hopeless— inmate. On top of this, these classes are administered, taught, and officiated by an officer, or a former officer turned case worker, with no more education or intelligence than some of the prisoners themselves. Most of these individuals are "teaching" these classes because they were ordered to do so by their boss. As a result, these teachers develop an apathy regarding the progression of inmates' characters that is impossible to conceal.

This focus on the average inmate and the appointment of poorly qualified and extremely indifferent instructors are the main reasons these classes are little more than spectacles. These two things are why these classes serve as spike strips, concrete barriers, sink holes, roadblocks, and massive twenty-car pileups along the incarcerated intelligentsia's road of opportunity. To refer to this as collateral friggin' damage is an understatement! These programs, as they are currently executed, prevent meaningful and measurable progress, hence the previously referred to "blockage." Yet, this doesn't stop them from being mandatory for inmates that wish to speed up the arrival of their release date.

To compound matters, prison administrations offer no significant assistance to the detainees that are capable of, and passionate about, self-education. As a matter of fact, at certain institutions the officials actually frown upon self-education. I have been threatened with disciplinary action for teaching other inmates about entrepreneurship. Prisoners are not given the opportunity to opine upon, critique, and possibly enhance a graduate student's dissertation, regardless of how thought-provoking their views and ideas may be. Detainees aren't encouraged to contact funders, write grants and draft proposals for non-profit organizations that they champion even though they've spent years following these organizations' actions, scouting potential supporters, and studying grant-writing techniques.

Inmates are dissuaded from writing business plans for non-incarcerated aspiring entrepreneurs in spite of the fact that, for them, the past decade consisted of little more than reading about business management and entrepreneurship, and dissecting and analyzing the specific industry into which the aspiring entrepreneur wishes to delve. Incarcerated individuals are misadvised from assisting financial advisors, low-level investors or brokers. Never mind the fact that some of them have spent the last twenty years doing nothing, scholastically, but monitoring their multiple imaginary stock portfolios. They're misadvised from lending their services to these professionals even though they've spent years evaluating financially informative literature such as major and local newspapers, investment/banking publications, independent assessments of commodity value fluctuations, analyses of emerging markets, and minutes from shareholder meetings.

One thing, however, is for certain: all penal system inhabitants in North Carolina, in order to avoid direct or indirect punishment, must sit in a room for three hours a week, six to twelve weeks at a time, and talk about why inmates should not stab correctional officers! In no way are these deprivations of opportunity and misguided applications of social control and rehabilitation productive. To be completely honest, all they do is piss us off and make us want to say "FUCK SCHOOL!"

Penal system officials respond to assertions such as this by boldly citing inmates' criminality and their perceived unintelligence as reasons to avoid restructuring these social toilets. A concept once expounded on by Carter G. Woodson comes to mind when I consider this response. When intelligent inmates begin to retrograde and adapt to their harmfully criminous surroundings, they are doing so because they are being deprived of every elevating influence. To put it mildly, inmates become "criminized" because they don't have any other *real* options in these non-reformative cages. When penal system officials (current supporters of longer prison sentences, very limited opportunities for the mental advancement of detainees, and excessively biased get-tough policies) are questioned about their aversion to penal reform, they respond by referring to the effects of these non-reformative environments as reasons to avoid rehabilitating inmates. When their responses are criticized, they resort to their old habit of answering their critics with the blood of assertion that the effort to enlighten and reform these possibly intelligent inmates would prove futile on account of their retrogression and criminous adaptation. In layman terms, these officials say they don't want to teach inmates to be *un*prisonized because inmates are already prisonized...crazy, right?!

These inmates are inured to hardships, surrounded by mental decay, viciously stigmatized, societally neglected, and subject to mistreatment by authority figures. The criminality that they develop as a consequence of these conditions is referred to as adequate evidence that they are incapable of transcending their lot. Their means of coping with their condition is evidence that they shouldn't be taught how to cope with their condition, and that any effort to teach them to tap into their potential, socially develop, and mentally excel would be productive of mischief both to the inmate and to prison officials. Because of this, the above-average prisoners are being pulled down into a trench of moral and intellectual gunk.

Inmates will not evolve until policy makers open a few doors for the most capable detainees, but policy makers say they refuse to open any doors because inmates haven't evolved!?! Prisoners will not blossom until officials re-design prison according to the needs of adept convicts, but officials refuse to re-design prison because prisoners have yet to blossom!?! This is such an ironic hindrance. And while this paradox is continuously being swept under the rug, the system's endorsement of ridiculously high recidivism rates is being collected into a societal dust pan, soon to be tossed into the civilizational recycling bin (which already contains Al Gore's Floridian votes from the 2000 presidential election, the missing tax-payer dollars that were sent to Iraq for "developmental purposes," and legal documents exposing the actions of the banking giants responsible for the 2009 recession).

What talent and intellectual prowess that does exist in prison is being wasted because the vast majority of researchers— and rehabilitative measures— are geared towards uplifting the VERY "un-upliftable." The most capable inmates are falling by the wayside because when penologists decide to conduct observational, statistical, and especially case studies, they're tricked into exclusively targeting the average inmate. There are tremendously deep reservoirs of talent, and even genius, sprinkled amongst the masses behind prison walls. However, ineffectively structured classes and personal development programs make these deep reservoirs look like shallow dirty pits. Also, when penologists ignore tools such as the one that you're currently looking at (this book), it effectively conceals what can be accomplished when the talent of these deep-thinking reservoirs is recognized, respected, and given hope and a purpose.

Unproductive Vocational Studies and Wasteful Leisure Time:

Penal system architects rely on information extracted from these fundamentally flawed case studies to design not only ineffectively structured classes and personal development initiatives but also leisure activities and recreational experiences. K.A. Cordes and H.M. Ibrahim noted a problem with these activities and experiences in *Applications in Recreation and Leisure for Today and the Future, Second Edition* when they inscribed the following: "...one of the reasons people are in prisons is because they fail to use their leisure time constructively and instead use it destructively. Initially, leisure experiences were included in correctional rehabilitation programs only to serve as an outlet for inmates' tension, frustration, and anger.

"Over time, however, it has become clear that incarcerated persons need appropriate guidance to help them make constructive use of their free time. Without leisure counseling, recreation programs for inmates may be either ineffective or actually destructive. As one criminal justice educator commented, 'prisoners come in, pump iron, and go out stronger than ever, often committing the same crimes.' Moreover taxpayers increasingly are opposed to subsidizing 'health clubs' for inmate body building. They want programs that deter crime rather than indirectly promoting it."

Penological case study subjects, especially the delusional ones that are inclined to conceal their allegiance to the crime-life, will not, nor cannot, convey the harm that is being done by prison activities as they currently exist. At the prison at which I'm currently housed, for example, the most common leisure experiences amongst detainees— experiences that do not include television— are playing basketball and volleyball, "pitching" horseshoes, strength training (lifting weights), and cardiovascular exercises (calisthenics). The only classes that are offered are those that allow inmates to get their General Education Diploma (GED), or more commonly, a particular construction-related vocational certificate. To an outsider this may seem reasonable and appropriate. Some may even believe that prisoners are lucky to have these recreational and educational resources.

Herein lies the problem. Most inmates are incarcerated for the following reasons: their use of physicality as a means of conflict resolution, excessive displays of physical aggression, thoughtless pursuits of physical pleasure, equating the lawful satisfaction of their needs with extreme physical exertion, or because they believe that prestige and "status" is determined according to one's physical capabilities (a belief that makes the possession of firearms quite appealing). Basically, their current misfortunes stem from their deep-seated physical orientation and an overestimation of the importance of physicality. (Although my focus right now is on physicality, I don't want you to forget that environmental factors that discouraged meaningful mental development, prevented the learning of "new" values or concepts of morality, and limited the exercise of their minds also played a role in landing many inmates in prison.)

Yet here in this prison, the previously mentioned recreational and educational resources that inmates use most often do nothing to address this. To the contrary, they promote an even heavier reliance on physicality. Construction trades and the aforementioned recreational activities indirectly harden and deepen what is already a problematic and thoroughly ingrained alignment with physicality.

Neither brick masonry, plumbing, electrical wiring, horticulture, playing basketball, playing volleyball, lifting weights, doing push-ups, power walking, nor pitching horseshoes teaches prisoners how to think critically, constructively, creatively, or comprehensively. All of these things center on physical work or physical "play" without regard for productive thinking, and the classes that are intended to teach inmates to think in this way are, as I've already stated, quite ineffective. This is very unfortunate because the possessor of an independent and flexible mind that is taught to operate and solve problems analytically will find recidivism as repulsive as sewage. Obviously teaching of this nature is non-existent behind prison walls. (Plenty of prisoners will readily admit to enrolling in, and completing, a series of prison classes THE LAST TIME that they were incarcerated.)

The randomly selected "average" inmate will never address this issue in this harsh of a light because it will require him to confront and scrutinize his personal beliefs, a confrontation that he isn't willing to have.

This average inmate cannot highlight the harmfulness of exalting physicality because he, himself, has spent his entire life doing just that. Admitting that this can be harmful means he must also admit that the beloved environment in which he was raised, his personal ethics, his parents' teachings (if such teachings exist), and the foundations of his value system are all tremendously flawed and need to be deeply examined and torn apart. He will never do this willingly; whether or not he's even capable of doing this is debatable. This supports the argument that sole reliance on the average inmate for case studies (or informational purposes in general) is ineffective, unproductive, and it doesn't assist pro-habilitation penologists in accomplishing their goals.

Get Tough Policies and Prison as a Crime Deterrent:

Cordes and Ibrahim also wrote that an "increasing number of individuals, communities, and governments are adopting get-tough policies, strong new anti-crime programs, longer prison sentences, fewer paroles, and fewer frills for prisoners" in response to taxpayers' stance against crime promotion and their desire for institutional crime deterrences. Yet these get-tough policies, along with prison scholastic programs, reformative measures, and the current state of prison recreational activities, constantly fail to accomplish anything substantial. Failing is really the only option that's available, as long as the creators of these initiatives continue to believe in disproven falsehoods such as the idea that the average inmate is the cornerstone around which widespread prison reform should be built and that the threat of future punishment steers criminals away from crime.

Supporters of this latter inaccuracy don't seem to understand the nature of crime. They appear to be unaware of the fact that criminality is mostly birthed by impulsiveness, a lack of true foresight, and incognizance of available opportunities. This kind of unawareness usually translates into backwards thinking, like digging up a flower and then complaining that its roots are not in the ground properly. Those that claim that the threat of future punishment is a crime deterrent seem to love such backward thinking though. Probably because they have their positions strengthened by ill-gotten case study findings that show that an individual inmate verbally claims to want to avoid crime in the future because he fears the possible consequences. (I hear this from delusional inmates all the time.) However, the behaviors that these backward-thinking falsehood supporters don't see usually fail to coincide with this inmate's proclamations. He's sort of like the person that secretly smokes a pack of cigarettes everyday while claiming that cancer is horrible and he hopes to avoid it.

This individual inmate's progressive façade may lead to the conclusion that get-tough policies, longer prison sentences, and recreational, rehabilitative/educational programs as they currently exist are reasonable means of reducing crime and recidivism. This fake image of himself— which is likely to surface when he's the subject of a case study— will support the lie that recidivism will decrease to the extent that inmates are subjected to these policies and sentences, and take advantage of these allegedly habilitative "opportunities." Incarcerated Thinkers have a very mature, classy, and sophisticated way to refer to lies such as these: bullshit! Thoroughly inaccurate BULLSHIT!

Yet and still, regardless of how we refer to it, and regardless of how many testimonies and how much data confirm the emptiness of these programs and ideas, the previously mentioned advocates continue to undergird these kinds of counterfactual beliefs. They seem to be unaware that these beliefs came from the practice of assessing average inmates. Also, penologists seem to be unaware that this practice causes them to overlook the Frommian idea that most human (inmate) behavior is a learned response to social (prison) conditions.

It has been theorized that people act out the behaviors expected of them by their society. This theory has much support in academia (notably Stanford University's prison simulation experiment) but remains disconnected from prison habilitative programs. In volume four of the *World Book Encyclopedia, 2006 Edition*, it states that "[d]uring the 1900's, criminologists proposed a wide variety of theories about crime. Edwin H. Sutherland, an American criminologist, developed the *theory of differential association*. It states that all criminal behavior is learned through association with criminals or people with unfavorable attitudes toward the law. Other criminologists believe the structure of society leads some people to choose criminal methods to achieve such socially approved goals as wealth and status. Still others argue that society produces crime, and so crime can be reduced or eliminated only by changing the organization of society," not by unproductively blaming inmates for not putting weak reformative measures to good use nor by enacting tough-on-crime policies and longer prison sentences.

To an inmate, these policies and sentences are just society's way of saying "We expect you to be a criminal." And considering the theory of differential association and his very criminogenic surroundings, he'll likely find it hard NOT to fulfill this expectation. There are a few criminologists and penologists that recognize this. (Google *convict criminologists* for some examples.) They consider this reality as they think logically and progressively about ways to reduce crime; too bad they haven't been given a platform from which to shout. Theirs is the voice of reason, and widespread criminal reform will materialize only to the magnitude that their positions catch traction and accelerate.

Crime-Producing Environments:

The position that holds the reorganization of society as the only significant method of crime diminishment is one that is viewed as valid by many well-informed studiers of this issue. (Criminologist John Hagon springs to mind here.) There are thriving environments in this society that are currently serving as havens for current criminals and breeding sites and training grounds for future criminals. (At least this is what can be gathered from analyzing current detainees; the argument can be made that crime occurs in all subsets of society with relatively equal frequencies and that the law enforcement system— unable to focus on all of society because of a lack of resources— simply chooses a subset on which to concentrate. More often than not, the "chosen" subsets are poor minority communities.) If a police department begins to incarcerate a magnanimous number of current criminals as a response to a particular get-tough policy, these criminals will surely be replaced by the younger products of these criminal breeding grounds. This is because the very environments and living conditions are instilling criminality into the youth, not the already established criminals.

Some inmates have in excess of four children residing in these particular environments, and this points to the future spread of criminality. (One would be foolish to believe that the existence of these environments is limited to the "Million Dollar Blocks" designated by the Justice Mapping Project; "Million Dollar Block" is a term that indicates the amount of money spent by the state on incarcerating people from these areas.) A governmental surge of incarceration of current lawbreakers may cause the crime rate to go down temporarily— and prison populations to soar— but the rate will surely rise again when these future criminals come of age. The extent of this societal dilemma can be well-concealed by the individual subject of a penological case study— the randomly selected average inmate— because this subject, himself, doesn't view it as a dilemma but as the natural progression of lives that are being lived by almost everyone that he knows.

For this reason— and many others– penologists should think deeply about who they choose to be case study subjects, and whether or not they are relying too heavily on these case studies to begin with.

PART TWO

**THE ILLUSION OF
REHABILITATION:
NORTH CAROLINA DEPARTMENT
OF PUBLIC SAFETY/DIVISION OF
ADULT CORRECTION—PRISONS'
EDUCATION PROGRAMS**

*(*The Illusion of Rehabilitation *was originally written to address certain prison conditions with which I am plagued. In 2012, a version of this literary creation was entered into multiple writing contests to no avail– "The Yale Law Journal Prison Law Writing Contest" and "The Eaton Literary Agency Writing Contest" to name a couple. It was also submitted to other sources with hopes of seeing it published, an example being www.occupyourstories.com. Unfortunately, this also turned out to be fruitless. I decided to include it here in its entirety so that you could have a more complete and comprehensive critique of prison reformative initiatives from my perspective. In accordance with Part One,* The Illusion of Rehabilitation *highlights the necessity of designing prison education standards according to the needs of the most intelligent detainees– also known as Incarcerated Thinkers. It also outlines complements to the current prison education model after explaining this model's failure to enlighten inmates on a mass scale. This explanation is sure to enrich my argument that habilitative practices are in dire need of reform and restructuring. I humbly ask you to pardon any aspects of the ensuing text that were already covered extensively in Part One of this book and trust that these aspects are more than worth repeating.)*

Many people believe that North Carolina's penal institutions are structured around the concept of rehabilitation. They assume that punitive confinement and seclusion are effective ways to discourage criminous behavior and combat illegal activity. I've even heard a proponent of mass incarceration state that prisons and jails are tools that are used to educate lawbreakers and habilitate– through forced "corrective" measures– the human agents of illegality. This mass incarceration proponent either had ulterior motives, or he was speaking from a position rooted in misinformation when he made this statement, as skyhigh recidivism rates can attest.

Regardless of whether his motives were impure or whether he was simply misinformed, I think that the more significant issue is the fact that this proponent's statement was merely a regurgitation of the rhetoric that most prison "outsiders" readily swallow and digest. This speedy digestion is mind-boggling to me, by the way. How can people that have no experience with, or accurate knowledge about, prison life and "inmate-ism" in general have the most firm and deeply rooted beliefs regarding current and former convicts? They have no problem appointing themselves to positions of penological authority, even though they are so misinformed. (This is evidenced by how they view prison's inhabitants and by how they treat these inhabitants upon their release from confinement.)

Sometimes these outsiders, these "prison aliens," cling hard to untruths. For example, they may directly or indirectly state to an ex-convict that "I'm not going to seriously consider your input because you've been to prison yet you're *still* rough around the edges." This statement implies that prison is a place that offers tools that smooth such "edges" and that this ex-convict simply chose to not take advantage of these tools while he was incarcerated. It also means that this ex-convict will not be permitted to explore an issue or analyze a problem until he first disproves this alien's opinion about him.

This is almost an impossible task because in this alien's opinion, if the ex-convict drives over the speed limit by two miles per hour, or uses a salad fork to eat steak, it's evidence that this ex-con didn't "learn his lesson" in prison (as if prison is a place where such "lessons" are learned). In response to such common but minor missteps, the alien will also declare that this ex-con is still in need of intense incarceration for a long period of time. This ex-con must carry this burden and argue for and defend his humanity– including his ability and capacity to reason logically, think coherently, and write lucidly– before he can even begin to live his life. He will remain preoccupied with carrying this very heavy weight, which is placed on his shoulders by "prison-illiterates," and this weight, which determines the content and character of his intellectual and moral activity, becomes unbearable when it's loaded on top of the massive cargo that is everyday living.

If you are a prison alien, you may be thinking that this "weight" is really a non-issue. You may even be thinking that an ex-convict deserves to carry this weight, and if he doesn't like it then he shouldn't have committed a crime. This is exactly what the typical prison alien would be thinking, but the typical prison alien doesn't realize that this particular stance is one big fat endorsement of crime. I'll get back to this later. For now, I want to keep your thoughts on the ex-convict who has already served his time (but will never repay his debt to society).

In addition to the huge boulder which is the task of proving his humanity to prison aliens, the ex-convict also has to guard against other artillery that gets fired by these prison-illiterates. For example, if he shows a little aggression, passion, or assertiveness, and unapologetically fails to flatter and lessen prison aliens' unease and discomfort, he's attacked by these penologically ignorant outsiders. The most common attack he experiences in such a situation is verbal; it's somewhere along the lines of "Although I've never heard of, nor interacted with you or anyone like you, I fear you and it's your fault. You're responsible for my fear so you should be alleviating it....Oh, you disagree? You're not sorry for not lessening my fear of you!?! Really!?! You should be held accountable....Oh, you disagree with this too? Well you are not capable of becoming a prolific citizen because you're unable to recognize or ascertain the consequences of your *existence* as such."

These beliefs, inclinations, and assumptions are extremely popular. Very few people, however, are aware of, let alone fully understand the fundamental issues and the foundational systemic circumstances that make these beliefs, inclinations, and assumptions almost completely erroneous, misguided, and counterfactual. Being oblivious of the fact that most people's view of prison's structure is based on misinformation is a rule with too few exceptions. Plainly speaking, nobody in power– from the collective laity to legislators to penal system architects– know that their perception of prison is wrong. This lack of knowledge is ubiquitous and unknowingly endorsed by a vast array of people because an overwhelming majority of citizens in our great nation are penologically ignorant. Up until now, the few people that really are penologically informed have been voiceless.

My goal for *The Illusion of Rehabilitation* is to scream this voice in your mind's ear. My goal here is to disclose and debunk popular sentiments, and to educate the penologically ignorant. People like me need to really make people like you aware of the non-(if not anti-) restorative nature of the North Carolina Department of Public Safety/Division of Adult Correction-Prison's (NCDPS/DAC-Prison's) education programs. There are many avenues that I could've taken to accomplish my objective and fulfill my aspiration, but I've chosen to focus exclusively on the "road" of prison education.

In the following text I will highlight this road's potholes, lane changes, construction zones, and detours. More specifically, I will address what is arguably the most significant, yet consequential, aspect of imprisonment: illusory education and its marginalization of, indifference regarding, and/or assault against rehabilitation.

Scholastic Opportunity Denial and Misrepresentative Reporting

"[C]ontrol units are torture chambers where prisoners spend from 22 to 24 hours a day locked up in a tiny cell for long periods of time with a blinding light burning all day, no educational or other kinds of programs, and without proper medical and mental health attention... However, we can and should turn these torture chambers

115

into our universities, for the betterment of
ourselves and our oppressed comrades."
~ By a Florida prisoner, December 2010

This inmate's sentiments are far from a Floridian anomaly; his viewpoints are not unique to Floridian detainees. His experiences are widespread throughout the nation, specifically the state of North Carolina. Here in the Tarheel State, many inmates are subject not only to horrible living conditions, but also to a denial of access to scholastically progressive paths. The NCDPS/DAC-Prisons not only withholds tertiary education from Incarcerated Thinkers with lengthy sentences, but it also prevents thousands and thousands of academically hungry inmates from receiving the type of basic education that fuels habilitation.

Very few people can disagree with the fact that this sort of denial, withholding, and prevention is harmful and un-American. As a matter of fact, most penologists understand that forcing inmates to reside at facilities with absolutely no opportunities for academic augmentation— due to ineligibility or simply a complete lack of available educational programs— is not conducive to reducing recidivism and enhancing society. Unfortunately, despite such an absence of disagreement and such shared understanding amongst influential academics and movers and shakers, precisely this type of denial, withholding, and prevention, is a pervasive reality behind prison walls.

In every region, at every prison, on every yard, inmates are being denied a *real* education (regardless of what legislators, prison administrators, or the state's prison website tells you). Helping inmates transcend their criminous tendencies through abundant educational opportunities is a concept that has been fringed, receiving much less focus than unproductive forms of punishment. As a result, incarceration in North Carolina has become irrefutably synonymous with fruitless punition in the eyes of an informed minority.

(By "informed minority" I mean the Incarcerated Thinkers and convict criminologists who are living within the system, not just reading about it in a comfortable classroom.)

When an individual is accused of violating this state's rules he is confined within the boundaries of a concrete box known as jail. If this accusation is deemed substantive by the courts, this individual is sent to a barbed wire box known as prison. If he then violates the prison's rules, he is circumscribed by an even smaller box made of steel–solitary confinement.

Incarcerated Thinkers (amongst others) know that neither of these "boxes" are replete with in-depth counselors, decent mentors, positive social interactions, or practical educational opportunities. The state spends millions and millions of taxpayer dollars every year to operate these punitive boxes, but not a single dollar is spent on any bachelors degree program for inmates. There are about 3619 people being held in this last box alone right now (solitary confinement), but the state refuses to enable just one inmate (me) to get a university-level education. North Carolina obviously values punishment more than education and it has designed its boxes so that they possess nothing that really helps any "box dweller." Even worse, progression through these boxes is still viewed as rehabilitative by an ignorant North Carolina majority.

Regarding this latter "box" (solitary confinement), I should make my opinion clearer. My view of it is almost identical to that of political pundit George Will, believe it or not. In an article entitled "Solitary's Torturous Toll," he wrote that "tens of thousands of American prison inmates are kept in protracted solitary confinement that arguably constitutes torture and probably violates the Eighth Amendment prohibition of 'cruel and unusual punishments'...Federal law on torture prohibits conduct 'specifically intended to inflict severe physical or mental pain or suffering.' And 'severe' physical pain is not limited to 'excruciating or agonizing' pain, or pain 'equivalent in intensity to the pain accompanying serious physical injury such as organ failure, impairment of bodily functions, or even death.' The severe mental suffering from prolonged solitary confinement puts the confined at risk of brain impairment....[such] isolation changes the way the brain works, often making individuals *more* impulsive, *less* able to control themselves. The mental pain of solitary confinement is crippling: Brain studies reveal durable impairments and abnormalities in individuals denied social interaction. Plainly put, prisoners often lose their minds....And remember: most persons now in solitary confinement will someday be back on America's streets, some of them rendered psychotic by what are called *correctional institutions."*

Instead of being taught how to live comfortably within lawful parameters, inmates are being permanently debilitated; their ability to function in the free world is being eroded by a standardized, taxpayer-funded box. This exemplifies social absurdity.

It's akin to subjecting one's child to corporeal punishment for a misdeed without regards as to whether or not that child understands the extent of said misdeed, and why avoiding that misdeed is in everyone's best interest. The child won't know what he did wrong, why he's being spanked, how long the spanking will last, or whether or not the spanking is excessive. Eventually that child will begin to view its parent as a mean, mysterious, easily agitated, and unstable person that is to be avoided out of fear of spontaneous eruption.

That child will likely begin to believe that its parent is "out to get him" for doing something with which he sees no fault. (Also, this parent will be this child's example of adulthood, so he may begin to mimic this parent's behavior as he grows up.) This child's perception of its parent is a parallel to an overwhelming majority of detainees' perception of the criminal justice system's methods of rehabilitation— the most significant being through educational programs. This perception is most obvious amongst the more radical inmates. They not only see the justice system as vicious, unpredictable, and out to get them, but they also view this system's efforts to habilitate people as some type of cruel joke.

However, it isn't mandatory that these perceptions (that of the child and that of the detainees), lead to future transgressions. They can be circumvented, if not conquered, through the application of thorough counseling and positive guidance. Because this is so widely understood, many incarceration facilities give the appearance of offering significant academic programs to inmates. The administrators of these facilities don't want to be accused of not applying this popular principle. But my research, consultations, open dialogical exchanges, and personal experiences, have confirmed that these programs are nothing more than facades. Most of what the prison system tells the public about prison academic programs is far from the truth (which is that these shallow programs have been implemented simply to pacify the disconnected but possibly influential members of society that may one day feel compelled to scrutinize the non-rehabilitative disposition of the NCDPS/DAC-Prison's educational system).

If you don't believe me, I encourage you to consult with one of the many community colleges that oversee prison continuing education programs. Let these colleges know that you want to verify or disprove my assertions. You can even request data on the academic performances of inmates that have completed the courses offered by a particular college through a particular NCDPS/DAC-Prison facility. However, please understand that this is just another source of misinformation. Many community college officials responsible for regulating scholastic activities behind North Carolina's prisons' walls are unaware of, or deeply involved in, the primary means by which instructors and prison program directors "doctor the books," so-to-speak.

The reporting of inmates' scholastic endeavors to collegiate officials is done in approximately the same deceptive manner statewide. This reporting process is structured on ascending levels of testing, with each level being categorized and unassumingly labeled. However, incarcerated students are enslaved to this process in a way that neither fosters their intellectual advancement nor provides accurate or trustworthy data to the collegiate overseers.

Here's how it works: the first level of testing often consists of what's referred to as "unit tests." These tests are administered only to the pupils that have displayed undeniably a decent understanding of the subject matter, the pupils who are best poised to earn high scores. After receiving such high scores on this first level, these students are herded into the next level of testing. This second level consists of what's known as "pre-practice tests." Students must score well on these tests before they're promoted to the third level of testing– "practice tests." Only a passing grade on these practice tests is required for students to be elevated to the fourth level of testing, a level which involves the completion of a "pre-test."

This fourth level of testing (the pre-test) must be completed and executed to the instructor's satisfaction before the student can progress to the fifth and final level of testing. This last level is usually a vocational exam or the General Education Development (GED) test, and it alone is what is reported to the collegiate executives and overseers for analysis. All of the other tests are hidden from view and are rarely ever mentioned outside of prison's classrooms. Clearly, the first four testing levels are simply academic "cloaks" that are used to cover the prison education program's weakness and inadequacy.

The use of these cloaks also has unintended side effects (beyond the devised plan to filter out the inmates that would make the prison education model look bad in the college's eyes). The most obvious and significant side effect is incarcerated students' excessive focus on, if not obsession with, test-taking. These students often view high test scores as the ultimate and primary goal. Actually knowing the material is only important to the extent that it helps them get high marks. If they can cheat, scheme, or guess their way to good grades, then the idea of actually learning stuff won't even be considered. Their motto is "get passing scores by any means necessary," not "get a practical education by any means necessary."

This test-taking obsession stems from a curriculum that revolves entirely around testing levels. Incarcerated students are taught how to navigate through multiple-choice exams before they're even informed of the subject matter and the course's objectives. Also, upon failing a test, they're often forced to wait several months before it can be re-taken; and if they fail a test multiple times they will simply be demoted to a lower testing level— without a single adjustment to the information being imparted to these students or to the method of instruction. A focus on, or obsession with, test-taking is really the only logical consequence of adhering to a scholastic model that trains students to esteem the outer test-taking "shell" over their inner intellectual and academic "cores."

As I indicated earlier, however, incarcerated students' test-taking orientation is merely a side effect. There's a devised plan lurking at the root of this education model. This plan is to present only the best possible image of this education model to collegiate administrators, officials, and directors, while keeping the less flattering details and components well hidden. More plainly put, the only individuals that are allowed to take the GED tests or the vocational exams are the individuals that have already proven that they will get high scores and make prison classes look better than they really are.

These are the only students that are presented to the people who are in charge of prison education programs, and they're also the students who will make these programs look good and effective in the eyes of prison aliens. The other students, the ones that don't get "presented," are often enrolled in these programs for multiple years without showing one iota of measurable progress. Many of them drop out of the programs to end their frustration with ineffective instructors and continuous test failures. Of course they are kept very far

121

out of sight. Their "enrollments" are often undocumented and their test failures always go unreported. The evidence that proves that the prison education department reports only the best students to their collegiate overseers while concealing the low-performing others is very striking in this regard.

From the college's perspective, the educational programs at the prison are doing well because ninety-nine percent of the students that take "The Test" receive a passing grade. Meanwhile, the instructors and the program directors conceal the fact that only the most capable inmates— approximately the ninety-ninth percentile— are allowed to take "The Test" in the first place. There's no wonder that the community colleges continue to misrepresent the prison academic program, an intellectual wasteland, as a well-oiled scholastic machine. So if you think you'll get accurate data from these colleges, think again.

One is hard put to find an example of another domain in which this practice of exposing the "good" and concealing the "bad" is not only accepted, but encouraged. A corporation once adopted this practice and decided to reveal only its impressive revenues (the good) to shareholders while concealing its towering and cumbersome debt (the bad). They weren't looked upon with kindness when this practice was revealed. Many people know this corporation as "Enron," and it serves as a despicable example of what not to do. How can Enron's actions be so strongly disliked, disheartened, and frowned upon, but the same actions when perpetuated by an alleged vehicle of enlightenment, are either ignored or explained away? Very few people can provide an acceptable answer to this inquiry. Very few people can adequately vindicate the actions of prison's scholastic system (as well as those of its overseers), actions consisting of blatantly obvious inaccuracies being delivered as gift-wrapped truths. The supervisors that receive these "gifts" get blinded by the opaque cloud of dust that arises when their watchdogs pat them on their hackneyed backs.

When analyzing statewide high school graduation patterns, would one only consider the district with the lowest dropout rate? When studying post-traumatic stress disorder amongst veterans, would it be sensible to ignore everyone that wasn't a jet engine mechanic? To measure accurately and report poverty levels, most can agree that focusing solely on upper management employees is illogical, unreasonable, and intensely misleading. It is undeniably deceptive, unethical, and immoral to portray the upper echelons, the highest achievers, as if they are the norm; as if they are the rule instead of the exception. Yet and still, a variation of these practices is unquestionably tolerated within the NCDPS/DAC-Prison's educational programs. Behind the closed doors of these programs, a small fraction of incarcerated students' testing performances are used to diagnose the quality and productiveness of the entire system. This is unacceptable, unproductive, and inconsistent with the American ideals that citizens have been taught since this country's genesis– namely hard work and honesty.

The Burden of Adept Detainees and the Provision of Online Education

Most facilities offer a General Education Development (GED) program to inmates that meet certain criteria. Not only are these programs misrepresented to prison aliens, but the structure of these programs is in disarray as well. Effective lecturing is unheard of and meaningful classroom discussions are non-existent. Instructors often relegate themselves to computer games and novel-reading when they are not reprimanding a pupil for what they have termed "disruptive behavior," which is nothing more than an inmate's pastime in the face of tediousness, inactivity, and ostracism within the classroom.

The tasks of educating incarcerated students (along with other pedantic responsibilities) are too often performed exclusively by other students. These "other students" are usually the most advanced pupils who are deeply concerned with the mental development of their fellow classmates. Of course, the execution of these pedantric responsibilities by these caring and considerate pupils is only accomplished if these pupils consciously decide to neglect their own academic enhancement and devote time and energy into assisting their less capable counterparts. This is viciously unproductive and intellectually abusive.

These elite and altruistic detainees are the least likely to become recidivists upon their release. In prison classes, however, they're forced to choose between two heartrending options, both of which have the potential to hinder their habilitation and make them more susceptible to post-prison criminality. The first option is to cling to their sociospiritual beliefs and tutor, guide, instruct, and aid their fellow inmates (because the need to do so is dire). But when these elite convicts select this option, they must ignore their own education and personal evolution to some extent, and this could make their habilitation more difficult and their re-entry into society more problematic.

These competent convicts could instead go the other route and select option number two. This option entails embracing selfishness, individuality and focusing solely on their own moral and intellectual growth. But when they choose this self-centered option they must suppress their sociospritual beliefs. If this suppression becomes permanent, narcissism would likely become ingrained in their psyches, and this would cause them to forever ignore the plights of others (part of the recipe for chronic criminality).

Placing this profound burden on the shoulders of North Carolina's most adept and considerate inmates is not a part of the recidivism-reducing recipe— especially considering that this situation is replicated in an overwhelming majority of prison vocational programs. The structure of these programs, which are offered behind the fences of North Carolina's "penal colonies," hardly differs from that of their General Education Development counterparts. (By "structure" I mean questionably qualified instructors indirectly forcing ignorant students to instruct their even more ignorant classmates while the system makes it all look like things are running smoothly).

With regard to the Incarcerated Thinkers, and others who proudly identify themselves as autodidacts, there is an effortlessly achievable way to tailor convict education to fit their needs and educate their less capable peers. There's a way to improve these structures and mold the prison scholastic system so that it serves the educational interest of these prisoners as well as others who actively delve into the Life of the Mind (i.e. those that cultivate intellectual activity). This molding would uplift all inmates in myriad ways, and it entails the implementation of online instruction programs.

Thanks to companies such as Flat World Knowledge, instructors now have access to affordable and customizable digital textbooks. These pedagogues can edit and remix their books' content, choose among versions, and move to new editions on their own schedules with unheard-of efficiency. Institutions have begun to take advantage of such access by publishing instructional content that is free to use, adapt, and distribute; a newly actualized trend that is known as *open educational resources.* Such flexibility and stream-lining would enable prison educators to teach convicts useful, applicable, and constantly evolving knowledge and skills if only they were permitted to incorporate such sources into the curriculum.

In addition to this instructional assistance, North Carolina's prison education model could also improve by granting convicts limited access to the internet.

Many for-profit higher education start-ups live in the "cloud," so-to-speak. This means they offer individuals high quality education via the internet. Examples include FortuneBuilders.com, CoachingOurselves.com, and Ben Nelson's *Minerva Project.* However, these elite internet education programs

125

can be priced far out of most detainees' financial range, and it would be unreasonable for me to expect taxpayers to cover the difference. (Limited access to post-secondary education in North Carolina prisons is made possible by The William and Ida Friday Center for Continuing Education at UNC-Chapel Hill, which will be opined upon later.)

Yet and still, I maintain that knowledge is still very free and ubiquitous in the cloud. This is thanks to organizations such as the North Carolina Virtual Public School, enterprises such as Khan Academy (which offers over 4000 free math and science videos for grade- and high-school students), platforms such as iTunesU, and schools like Stanford, Duke, and Yale that post thousands of lectures and lessons periodically. The efforts of non-profit corporations such as Creative Commons have also made tens of thousands of "open access" scholarly articles more freely available online— legally and within the protective contours of traditional copyright.

The most significant advances have been made by the providers of *massive open online courses* (MOOCs) such as Udacity and Coursera, both of which are on the path of gaining academic acceptance. This "path" is quite momentous, especially if one considers that over sixty prestigious schools of higher learning across the globe offer free collegiate level courses through Coursera's platform alone. This platform, along with Udacity and Udemy, Inc. (an online marketplace where instructors offer classes), is currently seeking recommendations from the American Council on Education. This should lead schools to further embrace MOOCs as legitimate vehicles for learning and grant credit for the successful completion of these classes.

Coursera and their rival EdX – founded by Harvard University and the Massachusetts Institute of Technology — are beginning to roll out proctored exams and web-based authentication tools to assess student performance. This latter enterprise has developed software that's capable of analyzing and grading advanced essays with the hope of lightening the workload of dedicated instructors. Through such initiatives, these MOOC providers are effectively combating the claims of college officials and administrators who think it is difficult to verify that students learn anything in these courses. Although many of these colleges and universities are rushing to offer these free online classes, they have a major financial incentive to limit academic credit only to registered, paying students — and not to those following along for free online.

Informative and insightful blogs such as Signal vs. Noise, educational networks such as ePals and Koofers, and businesses such as LearnUp.com also actively nourish mental activity and cerebral exercise on the web. It would take very little for inmates to be given access to these resources, and doing so would serve as a tremendous improvement to the current academic climate behind prison walls.

The North Carolina Department of Public Safety/Division of Adult Correction-Prisons should partner with the William and Ida Friday Center for Continuing Education to replicate the University of Wisconsin's Flexible Option program, along with expanding access to massive open online courses and open educational resources. This program offers multiple competency-based bachelor degrees from the state's public university system. It awards these degrees based on knowledge— not just class time or credits. It allows people to take a sequence of tests to prove their mastery of a subject without requiring classroom time and excessively high tuition. (This is also known as the College Level Examination Program– CLEP– throughout academia.) These assessment tests, as well as the related online courses, are written by faculty who teach the related subject-area classes; an arrangement which ensures and preserves this model's authenticity and eliminates the risk of dilution.

Molly C. Broad, president of the American Council on Education, agreed that such a program is "quite visionary." Kevin Reilly, president of the University of Wisconsin system says that such a program "is a big idea...and it is a manifestation of the way that the ground is shifting under us in higher education." Borrowing words written by Frederick Hess and published in the *Wall Street Journal* in an article regarding for-profit education, it's obvious that "what once required extensive resources can now be delivered faster, more cheaply, and more effectively using new tools and technology," and nothing other than laziness, ignorance, and subtle classism is preventing such progression from infiltrating prison's walls.

Implementing such a Flexible Option program (or CLEP) and allowing inmates to watch and listen to college lectures and take college courses for free via the internet would result in profound and relatively instantaneous reductions in this state's recidivism rate. Yet this will not occur unless educators, state legislators, and prison administrators detach themselves from romantic and oppressive conceptions of rehabilitating prisoners. Inmates and society at large will be well served if policy makers recognize that evolution is inevitable and that prison reform is possible. Here in this state, public and private organizations and non-profits that offer online instruction and scholastic advancement have vital roles to play behind prison walls when it comes to providing sufficient schooling for North Carolina's 35,000+ captives.

I have been housed at an institution where officials regularly gathered over one hundred prisoners— including myself— and escorted us to an on-site gymnasium to watch a movie shown on a projector. (There were even a few occasions when popcorn was served.) What prevented the administration from showing a college lecture in this same format? What is stopping North Carolina prisons from allowing interested detainees to view footage of college debates, footage that is freely available over the internet?

Why hasn't the NCDPS/DAC-Prisons designated a specific time, like every Friday, for inmates to watch a seasoned professor analyze and dissect an aspect of his or her field of interest? Why can't inmates regularly witness a skilled orator discuss relevant topics via an online "webinar," or a chief executive officer explain his corporation's activities at a shareholder meeting that's broadcasted over the internet? And what about TED Talks? Why can't we watch them periodically? Inmates aren't privy to the insightful and knowledgeable critiques of current events given by established social activists at speaking engagements. One can only respond to this iniquity with a not-so rhetorical "Why not?"

Such provisions require little to no extra resources, but their impact on prison reformative initiatives would be undeniable. This is a fact, not just mere posturing. It's well known that relevant and applicable schooling works miracles when it comes to rehabilitating detainees and miscreants in general. Differing fields of study from economics to socioculturalism agree with this and recognize the importance of administering practical education.

Concerning the former, and as noted in "Crime and Punishment: An Economic Approach", by Gary Becker (published in the *Journal of Political Economy*), microeconomists treat schooling as the largest component of one's "human capital." According to them, this determines one's labor market position by setting the level of his or her productivity. Simply stated, they believe school achievement, or lack thereof, is mostly what identifies what one is or is not capable of producing. This means that inmates, the majority of whom are high-school drop outs, are capable of producing very little and are thus marked early for low-paying and insecure jobs. (Economists of the secondary market school, which will be defined later in this text, refute this claim by pointing out that social and societal factors such as discrimination distort this process.)

Many studies have confirmed this schooling/human capital relationship. Such studies have verified the notion that labor market returns, attributable to schooling, are less for uneducated

129

(disproportionately minority and inner-city/at-risk) youth than for more educated (disproportionately majority and affluent or suburban) youth. Many experts support these findings and stand behind the notion that the more educated one becomes, the more he or she contributes to society's coffers. Likewise, they maintain that the less educated someone is, the more he or she subtracts from these coffers.

Additionally, it has been argued that schooling performs a variety of sociocultural functions as well. The most significant of these functions pertain to custodial and socialization provinces. We're in custody, so why not allow us to socialize with education advocates? Why not expose us to non-criminals in an academic setting so that we can truly learn how to not be criminals ourselves? Theories posited by socioculturalists such as Albert Cohen, Travis Hirschi, D. Elliott and H. Voss support the idea that school is a perfect way to accomplish this. Socioculturalist Mercer Sullivan once stated that "schools shape attitudes toward authority and adaptations to life in organizations as much as they imbue individuals with productive scholastic skills."

Considering these viewpoints of economic and sociocultural fields of interest, most can agree that giving inmates realistic access to contemporary and relevant sources of education is vital for them to make positive contributions to society. Such access is the key to teaching them how to avoid recidivism. As previously stated, the impact of the provision of relevant and advanced educational sources is not a secret; it's not knowledge to which I alone am privy. Multiple independent studies support my position on the effects that intellectual advancement has on reoffending.

One such study found that there was only a fifteen percent reoffending rate for New Mexico inmates who had completed at least one year of college, compared to sixty-eight percent for the general population. A separate study found ZERO recidivism for college graduates versus a reoffending rate of fifty-five percent for the general prison population at a California prison.

A third study conducted in the Midwestern United States reported that NONE of the first two hundred Indiana reformatory inmates earning a college degree offered by a university extension program returned to the reformatory after being released. For North Carolina to continue to neglect what other states have repeatedly identified as authentic means of reducing return visits to prison is nothing less than a disservice to taxpayers and a betrayal of statehood, state pride, and national patriotism.

Johnson Correctional Institution in Smithfield, North Carolina (the prison at which I am currently confined), does not allow detainees to view the History Channel, the Discovery Channel, or Public Broadcasting stations. Online educational initiatives are definitely out of the question. "The Young and the Restless," "Cops," and "The Maury Show" are, however, top priorities. This must change.

This system must discontinue its current practice of sheltering inmates from scholastically productive measures. Instead, it should encourage its captives to bask in the well-spring of education and intellectual life that is becoming more and more popular on the web. Andy Hines, a futurist who teaches at the University of Houston, sees opportunities in online programs for professional certifications and in "catch up" degree programs for people who started college but didn't graduate. These are opportunities that convicts should have. They have made their need for enlightenment abundantly clear by causing trouble and societal ills due to their lack of meaningful education, so why not give them access to these sorts of trends?

Denying such access is tantamount to criminality promotion. The current practice of completely ignoring the more intellectually advanced inmates, while failing to educate the average inmates, increases the chances that all inmates will one day relapse into criminal behavior. This practice will disappear when online education is made available behind prison fences. Instead of being neglected, the advanced detainees would receive the type

131

of attention that is most conducive to their mental progression. They would have access to the type of resources that most contribute to their personal growth, access which, as I've previously stated, they are currently denied. Eric J. Becoats, superintendent of Durham Public Schools in North Carolina, recognized the importance of further heightening the intellects of the most ripened pupils when he wrote "advanced students need advanced opportunities to maintain their momentum...we [need to] continue to differentiate instruction and provide additional resources and enrichment to advanced students."

Mr. Becoats understands the harm that could result from forcing the most mentally elevated students to learn the same material in the same manner (especially at the same pace with the same resources) as the less capable and further behind pupils. This specific understanding can easily be obtained by accurately analyzing the prison education model. This awareness of harmful practices can be made real by looking deeply at prison schools, where recent college graduates are forced to review basic addition and subtraction right alongside remedial sexagenarians with second grade educations. This is the place where former high school teachers have no other option but to sit in a classroom with dropouts whose intelligence quotients barely exceed highway speed limits and be forced to view picture books that explain the differences between a rectangle and a trapezoid. This is simply an atrocious distortion of the Montessorian method's use of group work for elder primary school students; yet this distortion is void of the educator's presentation of material, the aiding of students in independently exploring said presented material, and the final reporting of the student's findings.

Making online instruction available to inmates is a logical and achievable step towards inmate reform and recidivism reduction. Unfortunately, this step has yet to be taken, and even worse, the North Carolina Department of Public Safety/Division of Adult

Correction-Prisons regrettably seems averse to taking it for reasons that have yet to be made clear.

Misplaced Focus, Useless Curriculum and Fifth Grade Inmate

My position on prison education echoes that of Booker T. Washington, who was an esteemed educator in both the antebellum and post-Civil-War south. In "Education of Mind, Skill of Hand," he wrote about developing the famed Tuskegee Institute, and he shared some thoughts to which I can now relate. I'll borrow from him by saying that it seems perfectly plain to me, as it once did to Mr. Washington regarding southern Blacks, that here is a condition of things that cannot be met by the ordinary process of education. Decision-makers, alongside prison pedagogues, need to be convinced that the thing to do is to make a careful systematic study of the condition and needs of inmates. Then prison authorities should "bend their efforts in the direction of meeting these needs; whether they're following a well-beaten track or they're hewing out a new path to meet conditions probably without a parallel in the world."

Although I believe this would be the most productive route of action, I must be clear regarding my stance on inmates' individual responsibilities. I must state emphatically that prisoners have a moral obligation to bloom wherever they are planted, to the best of their abilities. Part of this "blooming" is fulfilling their societal duty to become better fathers, husbands, and men, regardless of what opposes such betterment. I am adamant about, and not seeking to decrease the significance of, personal responsibility on behalf of detainees. I believe that an inmate's personal aversion to self-actualization should not be a burden that this inmate can simply pass along to penal system educators and administrators. In other words, it is not my intention to completely absolve inmates of blame for high recidivism rates and leave non-incarcerated decision-

133

makers with the sole responsibility for convicts' education and post-prison lives.

In this context I recognize that an interactionist's approach– one fused with *mutual* sacrifice and effort– is necessary to actualize inmate reform (the same approach taken by Geoffrey Canada in spearheading the Harlem Children's Zone, and by Tim King in developing Chicago's Urban Prep Academies). This approach accounts for the fact that recidivism has multiple sources. The recently released ex-convict who violently seizes someone's platinum jewelry (and thereby injures himself as well as his victim) is one major source of recidivism. But so are the bankers, legislators, agents of criminal justice, employers, developers, and investors who have gotten rich creating an environment in which it is rational and appealing for this ex-convict to do the seizing. Multiple sources must be held accountable.

It is arduous, however, for some people to think about both kinds of accountability at the same time. This is why an in-depth outline of the ways in which inmates themselves should proactively pursue personal development and maturity will not be given here. This is also why my focus is on the flaws within the penal system's education program and the ways in which this system should be pursuing refinement and rectifying shortages and deficiencies that are obviously in need of rectification.

With this being said, I would now like to address the prison education model's center of interest, its focal point, if you will. This focal point is deserving of tremendous criticism. It is not one that aids in intellectual growth nor does it give the appearance of doing so. This point of focus, this nerve center, especially in non-vocational courses, pertains to the provision of relatively low-level diplomas and certificates.

The attention that low-level scholastic credentials receive in prison is grossly disproportionate to their significance beyond prison walls. Correspondingly, the neglect of meaningful mental progression within prison education programs is NOT indicative of its importance in the free society. A plethora of program administrators inadvertently highlight Adult Basic Education (ABE) certificates, General Education Development (GED) certificates, and even Adult High School Diplomas in a damaging way. The manner in which they concentrate on these low-level credentials leads detainees to believe erroneously that these accreditations alone separate from intellectual development, will counterbalance their felony convictions when it comes to their post-prison pursuit of financial and social stability.

This is quite problematic to ex-convicts. The baselessness of this belief is confirmed by the fact that millions have been released from incarceration with GED and ABE certificates, and/or high school diplomas under their belts only to be overlooked, ostracized, and neglected by job providers and ensuingly ignored, rejected, or exploited when pursuing loans, lines of credit, or start-up capital for any entrepreneurial aspirations.

It's no secret that, in prison, earning these less than impressive certificates is more important than the actual knowledge and intellectual wherewithal that these documents are supposed to represent. Too much praise is heaped upon a prisoner for "earning" his GED while inmates that exercise critical thinking or display analytical psyches are showered with nothing more than complete and utter indifference, if not antipathy. Seeing that such praise is given to inmates that successfully pursue what officials define as "education" (which is nothing more than certificate amassment), inmates understandably allow said "education" to get in the way of their learning. They concentrate on getting these imitation sheepskins and simultaneously shun mental development.

Note that mental exercise isn't required to obtain a GED. One must simply go through the proverbial motions and memorize formulas and test-taking techniques and he will be awarded a diploma. This absurdly pitiful structure— as well as careless and unreflective, yet commonplace instructors— makes it clear that mental development is not a vital component of diploma acquisition; therefore, it is often cast aside and sometimes seen as contradictory to the accomplishment of the inmates' goal. (The effects of such a miserably low "bar" will be outlined in the upcoming text.)

The result of such an arrangement is a system that regularly gives inmates diplomas and certificates while failing to adequately ensure that these inmates can comprehend the words that are printed on them. The reward system established to incentivize scholastic elevation behind prison walls is riddled with these sorts of inefficiencies. Academic programs should revolve around teaching students and the conveyance of meaningful, practical, and applicable data and information to these students. This distribution of senseless— i.e. distractive— pieces of paper shouldn't be a supreme goal. It's too bad this is not the reality within North Carolina's prisons. Concerning the latter conveyance of information, it's worth noting that no extensive attention is being paid to the actual curriculum in prison education programs. The material to which inmates are being exposed in prison classrooms is outdated, antiquated, inadequate and fruitless (and that's putting it nicely.)

If you don't believe me, consider talking to a few prison ABE or GED class graduates. After acquiring their low-level diplomas and certificates, significantly north of ninety percent of them have no idea what a 401(k) or an IRA is. They're thoroughly unaware of how banks and lending institutions operate and what bear and bull markets, bonds, ETFs, mutual funds, venture capitalists, angel investors, and leveraged buyouts are. They can't fill out a check properly, let alone read a balance sheet or fill out a loan application. They don't know what simple acronyms stand for (such as SBA or even LLC), and they can't define simple terms such as "mortgage" or "compound interest." Entrepreneurship is taboo, akin to an exotic ritual for most ABE graduates.

A tax credit, according to them, is something offered by VISA, American Express, and Discover.

Many that earn their GED certificate in prison also think that a person can earn a degree from the Electoral College if they just work hard and study. Of the thousands of organizations established to assist convicts with their re-entry into society, these diploma-earners can't name one. They believe that Warren Buffett has to be Jimmy's lesser known relative. I've conversed with many of these inmates, only to be surprised that they had no idea what Facebook or Amazon was.

Twitter was also alien to these guys— some, upon hearing the name of the social networking site, became frustrated when they couldn't find "Twitter" in the dictionary. They didn't know what an ISP was or did, and they had never heard of a search engine; they thought that Yahoo.com was a new version of some sort of chocolate milk, and that Google was a really long number. I've even had to violate prison rules by sneaking into a computer room to teach inmates how to play Solitaire just to get them more comfortable with using a computer mouse— they didn't know that computers had card games. Some of them have never seen a flat screen television before, let alone a smart phone; and they couldn't explain text messaging if their lives depended on it.

What's even more appalling is that some of these individuals were Generation X'ers that have only been incarcerated for about a decade and were mere days from being released in this complete state of ignorance! These "accredited" individuals were unequivocally and inarguably ignorant of the basic mechanisms that support modern humanity, staples of human evolution on which today's empires are built. Yet they were steps away from being free men. They had no idea how society operated, how power was obtained, nor how one should go about gaining more control over his or her own well-being. Yet they were just days from being heads of households. These graduates were absolutely clueless

137

regarding everything that truly matters in this modern world, not only concerning finances and technological progressions but also simple conversations, social interactions, child rearing, spousal unity, basic mathematical computations (they struggled with basic math problems that they didn't have committed to memory), and almost every other facet of productive societal existence.

Once again, another not so rhetorical question is due: what exactly does the curriculum in prison education programs consist of, and why is the answer to this question evading scrutiny? An extremely high percentage of people that earned their GED while incarcerated will come back to prison eventually, so what is being taught in these prison GED classes that could explain such inefficiency? What exactly are these guys learning if not the things that are most significant? What constitutes an Adult Basic Education?

A sky-high recidivism rate amongst students in prisons across the state should lead one to believe that the answers to these inquiries need examination. I have conducted such an examination and found that the curricula in prison scholastic initiatives, amongst other things, are both useless and asinine. I dare say that prison education programs are most skilled at teaching prisoners how to become recidivists, more so than anything else.

If your hair is standing up on the back of your neck, if my assertions have gotten you up in arms, then feel free to openly critique me. One route that you may take is to research the recidivism rate amongst those prisoners that complete these scholastic programs and compare this rate to that of prisoners that do not enroll in any type of academic program whatsoever while imprisoned. After doing this, you may use your findings to try to disprove me. You may center attention on the fact that some studies and reports show that about seventy percent of inmates relapse into criminal behavior within three years of being released, while this number drops to about sixty percent amongst the inmates that take part in North Carolina's prison education initiatives. You can present this finding in a way that supports the false notion that academic programs administered in this state's prisons are actually succeeding in productively educating detainees, and that a reasonable argument countering my assertions does exist.

I, however, am a friggin' intellectual boy scout and a literary ninja; expect me to be very prepared for your critique, and to strike back with mongoose-like reflexes. My first response to "your" critique (which is really what I think a regular prison alien's critique would be) would be to shine a light on its emptiness. This would be done with a couple of questions: 1) if sixty percent of ALL high school graduates were homeless and unemployable within three years of graduating, would the homeless and unemployability rates of those never enrolled in school have any bearing on the direness of reforming this nation's school system? And 2) if sixty percent of ALL service men and women committed suicide within three years of leaving the military, would the suicide rate amongst those that never joined the military detract from the need to conduct thorough investigations within this nation's armed forces?

The answer to both of these inquiries is a resounding NO. Likewise, this also applies to the effectiveness of "prison classes." The recidivism rate amongst convicts that do not attend school while incarcerated neither delegitimizes nor undergirds the abysmally high recidivism rate amongst convicts that do enroll in prison scholastic programs. Second of all, consider that the more intelligent individuals that get incarcerated (the ones that, at the onset of their imprisonment, are already the least likely to become recidivists) almost unanimously enroll in some sort of class while confined, and the claim that lower recidivism rates amongst the "credentialed" verify the effectiveness of low-level prison education is even less substantive.

But more importantly, why would you try to justify a sixty percent recidivism rate to begin with? Sixty percent isn't good, and all of the data confirms the notion that growth and mental evolution are not being nourished inside prison fences. So when you say that a relatively lower (sixty percent) recidivism rate for prison students means that prison classes are doing well, are you disregarding the fact that the creation of critical thinkers, the one thing that formal instruction is supposed to accomplish, is what is most ignored by prison education models? If this is your position, then you should be able to answer these tough questions.

If you're on my side, however, then you're probably asking other questions as well. Specifically, why aren't the academic problems being solved? Why isn't more emphasis placed on nourishing marketable skills and interests in prison education programs? Why is the NCDPS/DAC-Prisons' education model failing to instill in inmates the importance of thinking logically and sharply, of knowing how to conduct research, and of undergoing, applying, and capitalizing on employment training? This is what would reduce criminality and ensure this system's namesake (public safety), not their current practice of simply gathering and isolating convicted criminals. To succeed at instilling such qualities into inmates is to succeed at productive reformation and fruitful instruction and education (all components of enhancing true public safety).

So why is this success so elusive? This composition isn't meant to address this complex question in its entirety, but I will expound on a few education-related issues that should point you in the direction of a comprehensive answer. Taking what I've outlined thus far and combining it with one more often overlooked, yet consequential, education-related issue in particular, would be a good place to start.

This consequential issue is the systemic practice of encouraging prison instructors to approach inmate education myopically, unilaterally, and mono-pedantically, if-you-will. Or, as we Incarcerated Thinkers like to say, the system is telling teachers that there's only one way to skin a cat. The socially controlling punitive system herds prison teachers into teaching as if only one form or one education model exists– that of traditional and mainstream public education. The teachers behind prison walls are frequently trained to teach inmates basic elementary math (addition, subtraction, division, multiplication), reading (syllable and word identification, pronunciation, and literary comprehension), and writing (sentence structure and correct grammar and punctuation usage) in the same way that they would teach regular elementary school students.

Due to such training, this is exactly what these teachers attempt to do. They don't' acknowledge detainees' precarious plights and their very unique capabilities. They don't go the route of Defy Ventures— the MBA-style program for felons which was created by the wonderful Ms. Catherine Rohr (a lady on whom I happen to have a little-boy-like crush). Instead, prison educators instruct inmates as if they're regular fifth-grade school students– viciously violent, unsophisticated, primitive, and very untrustworthy fifth-grade school students, but fifth-grade school students nonetheless.

This perception of inmates isn't entirely accurate and when held by instructors, can be quite problematic. When teaching fifth graders, most teachers expect their students to have some measure of non-academic education. Teachers expect parents to have taught their children to respect authority, to have basic manners, and to know the value of treating their peers with courtesy by the time these children began progressing through public school. (Most of the worst performing students lack these parental teachings, but unfortunately elementary school educators can do very little about this). Primary school instructors believe that giddiness, high-energy levels, and short attention spans– all of which are common to fifth graders– should be the only things that would prevent a child from focusing entirely on his or her schoolwork.

They don't expect a child to be battling with unavoidable, multifarious forms of abuse. They don't count on their pupils being drug addicts who live under constant, and sometimes magnified, fear of violence. These pedagogues don't consider that on any day, they themselves could leave work in an ambulance with life-threatening injuries inflicted by a fifth grader. They don't assume that their students were recently snatched away from their loved ones and caregivers, and as a result, are constantly bombarded with mental images of their mothers, fathers, and/or siblings.

The possibility that these regular primary school students are haunted by gruesome images of stabbing another human being repeatedly, until only a bloody and vaguely recognizable corpse remains, is a variable that public school models don't encourage elementary school teachers to factor into their "teaching equation." These teachers also don't believe that the reason these fifth graders can't seem to focus in class is because they are forced to share a bunk bed with a proudly convicted child rapist every night; nor do the female educators fear getting raped by one of their pupils at the slightest provocation. Most importantly, these educators don't anticipate the likelihood that completion of the class gets these fifth graders one step closer to being rid of all of these aforementioned troubles.

Teachers of regular public elementary school students see these scenarios as absurdly far-fetched and unrealistic. Prison education models, however, must convey to prison educators the importance of viewing these scenarios as reality and adjusting their interactions with inmates accordingly. If the prison education model cannot be structured according to the needs of the most capable detainees, it should at least recognize the conditions of the average and below average detainees that it allegedly seeks to educate.

Even though many of these convicts have emotional maturity and intelligence levels equivalent to those of slightly precocious fifth graders, one would do tremendous harm in allowing this fact to color the way these inmates are taught and instructed. Simply put, adult convicts are not eleven-year-old fifth graders, and the model used to educate adult convicts should not be an exact replica of the model that is used to educate elementary schoolers. This latter "model" does nothing more than prepare students for the next level of schooling, a level that inmates will most likely skip as they're released from prison and hurled into full-fledged adulthood. Solely and exclusively applied methods of educating fifth graders will never adequately prepare underdeveloped adults for adulthood of this nature; therefore, the prison education model's framework should NOT completely mirror that of the public primary education model, as it currently does.

Elementary education processes alone cannot equip an adult with the tools that are necessary to generate a livable income and run an ergonomically sound household. Yet, this is the preparation that convicts need most, especially since the majority of them have relatively short sentences (meaning that they will be adults living in the free world sometime in the near future). The life skills that are NOT imparted by conventional elementary school systems are precisely the skills that a detainee must develop in order to contribute to societal evolution upon his departure from prison.

Educators within the penal system should not focus on mimicking elementary education models. They should be much more concerned with bridging the long-standing gap between formal primary academic instruction and practical, applicable, and commercial knowledge and skills. They should emphasize learning information that adults can use. For example, no logical and efficient adult education system should stress the development of an adult student's ability to do long division and ignore this student's ignorance of basic banking functions such as how to open and maintain a savings account or the difference between debit and credit. Yet this is exactly what adherents to the prison education model practice.

Gravitating towards such a sensible emphasis would begin the process of informing detainees that other options in life exist besides criminality. Tailoring

143

prison instruction to the needs of undereducated adults instead of to needs of children preparing for the next grade level would leave convicts poised to tackle adulthood legally, and with some measure of decency. Such tailoring would enable them to transcend what Bennett Harrison defined as the "secondary labor market."

In *Education Training and the Urban Ghetto,* Harrison maintained that the American society is not a single meritocratic society in which all individuals are equal competitors. According to his argument, there are at least two different American labor markets, or fields of competition, at work simultaneously at any given moment. The first of these fields is the *primary* labor market. This is where steady employment at relatively high wages supports families. The *secondary* labor market, however, is one in which low-wage jobs, welfare, employment and training programs, informal economic activities, and most importantly, crime, must be alternated and combined because none of these economic activities alone can provide a steady living.

Inmates that receive exactly what current prison education models here in North Carolina have to offer are destined for a life scraping along the bottom of this secondary labor market. Without proper instruction and access to a highway of education that leads towards habilitation, these inmates will exit prison and resort to a combination of odds and ends hustles, poor paying jobs, and significant involvement in illegality simply to survive with a semblance of respectability. Advanced and customized education is the key to changing such a destiny; modernizing the prison education model is the ticket that grants entry into a less harmful, law-abiding fate.

It's time for the NCDPS/DAC-Prisons to get serious about the safety of the public by actively and effectively educating and rehabilitating those who the system has identified as the biggest threats to said safety. Although my focus here is the NCDPS/DAC-Prisons, I must make it clear that this problem (the

144

astonishingly high recidivism rate amongst graduates of the educational programs definitely makes this system's scholastic structure problematic) is nationwide. This hidden disregard for the academic elevation of the incarcerated while promoting an image that implies otherwise is endemic in our society.

A California prisoner wrote in September of 2010 that "[t]he prisoners languish inside, trapped in a deplorable state of ignorance. Mental boundaries often go no further than the few city blocks of their own neighborhood's horizons. The illiteracy of the many would be laughable if it were not obvious that, for the most part, it is not self-induced. With no expectations that the captors will relent– for it is not in their best interest to do so– the captives must endeavor to enlighten themselves in an organized manner."

Myriad studies have verified the notion that the diminishment of physical aggression, the lessening of impulsiveness and the application of enlightened clairvoyance are all vital for the success of a released detainee. Studies have also shown that these three tenets are directly proportional to an inmate's level of education and scholastic development.

In agreement with the results of these surveys, the previously quoted California prisoner continues extolling the benefits of educating inmates by saying that "[e]ducated prisoners, when released, have not only more confidence, but they also possess greater opportunities of obtaining gainful employment. Obtaining real knowledge gives them the potential to aid in restoring economic value to families and communities. Educated prisoners also increase the pool of those who can become politically active to affect lasting societal change, and their chances of avoiding legal trouble increase as well...therefore educating prisoners will decrease crime and violence as incarcerated minds expand and deepen."

Academic Privilege Revocation, Meaningful Book Reports, Removing Obstacles

You may believe that there are academic programs available to all inmates, programs that serve as avenues of upward mobility. You may even believe that enrolling in said programs is a privilege, and inmates that violate certain rules should have this privilege revoked. The former belief, concerning the availability of academic programs, is thoroughly counterfactual and inaccurate. The latter belief, concerning the denial of privileges, is actually understandable, and I can see how a prison alien's vista would lead you to agree with it.

Nevertheless, if one is to operate on the notion that incarceration's purpose is to habilitate, then how could one sensibly view what scores of social scientists believe is the most effective means of habilitation– enlightenment, mental development, and academic improvement– as a privilege that can be taken away for the most minor infractions? Would diseased people expect to go to a hospital and be denied treatment if their illness manifests too intensely? Do middle-school students expect to receive detention if they are discovered to be unacquainted with the subject matter? Of course not, because hospitals are a place for the ill to be treated, and schools are a place for students to learn and become abreast of certain topics.

It's amazing that all can agree on this, but prison aliens still believe that prison's residents— "prison" allegedly being a place for lawbreakers to be remade and restored— should be denied access to scholastic programs for displaying certain behaviors. These behaviors are what made the courts deem their very presence in prison a necessity to begin with. They're in prison to correct and refine these immoral behaviors and unlawful tendencies, not to be continuously and unproductively punished for them. The entire inmate population should be on a path that leads towards reform, a path from which one shouldn't be able to be disqualified due to the behavioral problems that prison is suppose to be fixing.

One tool that can be used to put inmates on this reformative path, to complement the current system and customize convict instruction, making it available to ALL inmates, is literature. As of these writings, required readings are a non-existent component of this prison system's education agenda. Neither Adult High School Diploma, GED nor ABE programs amongst the imprisoned— or any other prison programs for that matter— require any sort of extensive reading (other than the three or four measly three hundred to three hundred fifty word essays that are read, and even these are never discussed nor openly opined upon outside the context of grammar and punctuation usage). This is quite appalling, considering the treasure trove of knowledge that lies between the covers of myriad books and the overabundance of "free" time that exemplifies inmate life.

All prisoners, regardless of their academic pursuit or enrollment status, should be required to submit a book report of a pre-specified length— possibly 1000 to 3000 words— for grading and assessment on a regular basis (annually or semi-annually). I'm not a big fan of having the threat of punishment over someone's head like the sword of Damocles, but in this context I can envision negative consequences being administered to the inmates that refuse. Complying with this requirement would lead to the expansion of convicts' literary and intellectual interests. Upon completion, it would also give them a sense of accomplishment. Working hard on such reports, harder than any GED or ABE class assignment requires, and being rewarded for their *effort*, not their presence, with a completed project would introduce them to the notion that work, real work, produces fruit.

These detainees should be required to select a book from a list of mostly nonfiction works that pertain to practical living, mental and emotional growth, and the development of proliferate skills and talents. This list should include autobiographies and biographies of individuals from all walks of life (from Andrew Carnegie and Marcus Garvey to Anne Frank and Steve Jobs), well-written "how-to" literature (such as The *Complete Idiot's Guide to Parenting* and *Starting a Business for Dummies*), and informative yet linguistically artful fiction written by authors such as Ayn Rand, Alice Walker, and Virginia Woolf. This list, by all means, should exclude the easy reads and senseless prose that public schools have passed off as "classics" for decades now. Inmates must not be exposed to the pointless literature which plagues this nation's public school systems.

In quoting proponents of the new required reading guidelines recommended by the Common Core State Standards in english, Lyndsey Layton of the *Washington Post* wrote that "U.S. students have suffered from a diet of easy reading and lack the ability to digest complex nonfiction including studies, reports and primary documents. That has left too many students unprepared for...the demands of the work place," demands that convicts must be able to meet upon their release in order to become productive members of a community.

It is well-known that children are completing grade-school without first acquiring important life skills such as the ability to make an argument supported by evidence, or the capacity to articulately and eloquently demonstrate a plan or an idea with something verifiable behind it. I believe that "easy reading" is part of the problem here. Inmates simply don't have the luxury of being deprived of such skills and capacities in the same way that easy reading deprives public school attendees. Convicts can't afford to be crippled by a primary public school model that neither trains students to be successful nor develops the kind of leaders that are poised to move this world forward. It's illogical for such a structure to serve as the framework for the prison education model.

The secondary education model isn't much better nor is it improving. The North Carolina Department of Public Instruction (NCDPI) found that the percentage of students having to repeat english, math, or reading in North Carolina community colleges following high school, increased from fifty-seven percent in 2007-2008 to sixty-five percent in 2010-2011. (This increase alone cost over eighty million dollars.)

This paradigm, this education model's framework, has a record that is much more lackluster when socioeconomic factors are factored in. Only fifty-four percent of socioeconomically disadvantaged students in this state (a category into which the bulk of detainees were thrust during their stint as students of the North Carolina public school system) passed the end-of-grade tests last year according to the NCDPI. It's also worth indicating that the achievement gap between poor students and their wealthier peers on these tests has increased. It's quite clear that the public school model and its easy reads don't favor the relatively impoverished, so why should it serve as the blueprint for the prison education model when almost all students in prison fall into this category?

Better yet, why try to educate inmates using a system that already failed to educate them when they were enrolled in public school prior to being incarcerated? Giving them more and more of what, for them, was a bad thing won't make this bad thing magically become good. (In keeping with my writings thus far, I must reiterate that inmates probably will not encounter a different and more productive education model after being exposed to the prison education model, therefore correcting the problems exacerbated by this model, the previously referred to "bad thing," is very unlikely.)

Convicts cannot afford to be plagued by these irrelevant distractions throughout their entire sentences. They don't have space in their lives for the public school model and its lame, mainstream American literature— *The Lord of the Flies* and *1984* have outlived their usefulness, run their course, and overstayed their welcome. These inmates must procure the aptitude that public schools seem to be averse to teaching in order for them to stay focused on what matters, to stay out of prison, and to endure adulthood. To aid in such procurement, it is vital for prison educators to avoid the sources of such distractions and shun ineffectual tomes such as *Animal Farm, Moby Dick,* and *The Scarlet Letter.* These so-called "classics" don't work for grade school students and they won't work for inmates...EVER!

Although selecting literature from a list of books that are more likely to "work" for detainees, and submitting a book report on said selection, should be a requirement, it should be accompanied by a merit-based reward system. There should be some sort of objectively operated system established at each prison which grants the writers of the twenty or so best reports a decent meal, or the opportunity to watch a recently released DVD, or maybe a special conjugal visit. (The advantages of conjugal visits, as cited in multiple studies, include the lessening of forced and voluntary homosexual acts within prison, the maintenance of a more civilized prison environment, the curtailing of harmful isolation from the outside community, the lowering of tension levels, the diminishment of attacks on correctional officers, the reinforcing of gender-appropriate roles, and the preservation of meaningful marriages.) Establishing such a systemic literary requirement, as well as a method of rewarding good work, would produce easily recognizable results in a relatively short period of time.

Along with such proposed mandatory literary initiatives, inmates could also be rehabilitated and reformed through enrollment in formal debate classes. If these classes were taught by intelligent and credentialed instructors, and proctored by qualified moderators, the incarcerated students would learn more than just effective debate practices and techniques. They would also learn self-control by exercising the articulate expression of their ideas while acknowledging, harnessing, and channeling intense emotions. They would be made aware of acceptable and effective conversational etiquette as well as the value of possessing a broad vocabulary— all through participation in a well-structured debate course.

Along with benefits like teaching the incarcerated how to interpret data, how to conduct research, where to gather needed information, and how to assess, filter, compile, and present such information in a way that makes sense, these courses would also promote and encourage critical thinking. If properly administered, these classes would teach prisoners how to handle disagreements in meaningful and fruitful ways (without automatically resorting to violence or being reduced to personal verbal attacks and insults). At the same time, their awareness of, and knowledge concerning, the topic being argued would increase. These classes would give detainees the opportunity to develop the skills necessary to objectively critique and analyze an issue, and utilize inductive and deductive reasoning with the hopes of actualizing a desired outcome.

The acquisition of such knowledge and the development of such interpersonal skills and communicatory abilities are solutions to some of the penal-related problems that are currently strengthening the roots of many individual inmates' criminous characters. According to the *National Policies on Corrections as Ratified by the American Correctional Association,* the Correctional Policy on Offender Education and Training states that "[g]overnmental jurisdictions should develop, expand, and improve delivery systems for academic, occupational, social, and other educational programs for accused and adjudicated juvenile and adult offenders in order to enhance their community integration and economic self-sufficiency. Toward this end, correctional agencies should....make available opportunities to participate in relevant, comprehensive educational, vocational, and social skills training programs and job placement activities that are fully coordinated and integrated with other components of the correctional process and the community as a whole....." There are no identifiable programs operating in North Carolina's penal system that are cheaper, more effective, easier to implement and manage, and more in accord with this guideline than a prison debate class coupled with the aforementioned book report requirement.

There are also very few substantial obstacles that cynics could use as reasons to avoid implementing this idea. Decent literature could easily be made available. There's a plethora of individuals and institutions that are willing to donate reading materials to prisons. I've conversed with prison instructors who say they know plenty of people that would make themselves available to read and evaluate book reports as the need to do so arises. (As previously stated, massive open online course provider EdX has recently developed a freely available computer program that's designed to determine the quality of collegiate-level essays. Thanks to such efforts, the need to evaluate book reports should never become overwhelming.) All prisons have the means of designating a "quiet zone" so that inmates can have a distraction-free area in which to write, read, and study. Problems stemming from scarcity of capital (i.e. fiscal shortcomings) can be solved through annual education grants or by utilizing financial services such as those offered through www.donorschoose.org, a website that facilitates aid to public school classroom projects.

Additional fiscal problems may be rectified by simply redirecting the funding that's allotted for the wasteful and pathetically barren programs that have been chugging along for years behind prison walls. The resources, monetary and otherwise, that support these wasteful programs could be applied to executing the aforementioned required reading and debate class initiative. Redirecting funds in this manner may meet undue opposition due to the fact that almost all of these inadequate and money-squandering programs are religious in nature. However, absolutely no data shows that these programs are successfully rehabilitating convicts nor that they're providing services that the inmates are unable of providing for themselves. Taxpayers should be paying for something that reduces crime— education— while allowing religious programs to be privately funded. This point alone should easily put this undue opposition to rest.

To keep it real, I find quite laughable, the shoulder-shrugging that occurs when one asks how such penological education proposals can be funded. There's a very lucrative way to generate the revenue that's needed to fund these scholastic propositions. It's actually quite obvious to anyone that's even remotely aware of prison, and it relates to the inmates themselves. More specifically, it's their high levels of inactivity.

There are thousands of healthy, athletic, drug-free men simply wasting away in North Carolina at any particular moment. These men do the prison equivalent of twiddling their thumbs day in and day out for years on end. Such a misuse of human resources is ridiculous; such a waste of prisoners' time in idleness is staggering.

Neil Singer conducted an analysis of potential inmate economic benefits in 1973 and found that 208,000 felons in prison could each earn an average of 8,038 dollars annually, or 1.67 billion dollars in total. Now, a couple of generations later, and with today's prison population of approximately 2.2 million, that amount could be estimated at closer to 17.7 billion dollars— or 281,330,000 dollars just amongst North Carolina's 35,000 captives alone— in 1973 dollars! (Adjusted for inflation, this number can be estimated at over 1.4 billion dollars today, here in this state every year.) Such economic realities should cause legislators, managers, and regular citizens to wince when they appraise current forms of treatment, especially considering this state's current financial problems.

Furthermore, America is no longer the manufacturing powerhouse that it was in the years following World War II. The term "Made in America" isn't emblazoned across products worldwide anymore. Quite the contrary; for years now, U.S. companies have been sending jobs to other countries for manufacturing purposes mainly because of the attractive (i.e. low) wages with which workers are allowed to be compensated in said locales. I suggest that instead of pursuing cheap labor overseas, American companies should operate with some measure of social responsibility and train and employ domestic detainees.

Giving prisoners marketable skills and a job that pays fifty, sixty, or seventy percent of the federal minimum wage is advantageous to all involved parties. It will not only keep labor costs low for businesses and generate tax revenue for the state, but it will also leave inmates suited to pay for their own educations while imprisoned and be released with useful skills and significant financial savings. (Not to mention the fact that MOOCs and a CLEP or a Flexible Option program would give employers a labor pool of skilled and college educated individuals from which to choose an employee— individuals eager and proud to work for as little as half of the minimum wage.)

With such an opportunity, these inmates would also learn how to document, budget and manage their income more productively. Such knowledge will enable them to make positive contributions to their households and communities upon their release. This currently isn't feasible due to the non-skilled jobs— paying just a few cents per hour— that are currently available within North Carolina's penal system. Convicts are released from prison with no employable skills (at least none capable of counterbalancing their felony convictions) and saddled with thousands of dollars in debt for restitution and probation, parole, and prison room-and-board fees. They're broke, in debt, and very unattractive in the eyes of job creators; they're akin to college graduates with student loan debt minus the education and the job training. This is a recipe for failure.

Based on extensive interviews, I've concluded that almost of all North Carolina's prisons are structured in a way that allows at least forty percent of their residents to do nothing beyond eat, sleep, watch television, exercise, and read. This means that each facility houses two, three, or four hundred strong and able-bodied men, aged twenty-five to thirty-five, with years and years of free time that basically gets wasted in idleness. We should allow this labor pool to help solve this state's fiscal woes, to send money home to buy food and school supplies for their children, and to fund their own education and training— literally, to re-pay their debts to society.

Instead of taking fifteen to twenty inmates off of prison grounds for eight hours to pick up trash alongside the highway for seventy cents a day, take these inmates to a construction site to build a home for a general contractor and pay them sixty percent of the minimum wage. Instead of forcing a few inmates to spend two days mopping already clean floors or dusting dustless shelves in order to purchase one postage stamp, Wal-Mart could hire these prisoners to sew Faded Glory jeans for four dollars an hour and replace "Made in Bangladesh" on the denims' tags with the once prestigious "Made in USA" insignia. (Companies such as Victoria's Secret that already employ American prisoners rarely pay these prisoners anything above forty cents per hour; such ruefully meager wages do not help inmates become decent citizens capable of providing for themselves.)

Those that believe harsh punishment is the most effective means of reforming delinquents— such "believers" are delusional anti-rehabilitationists by-the-way— may be against uplifting and empowering inmates in this way. They may think that prisoners should do nothing other than live in squalor while contemplating little more than the actions and activities which landed them in prison. According to these punishment advocates, inmates should not be allowed to receive any portion of the fruits of their forced labor, and they shouldn't be given the opportunity to pursue post-prison self-sufficiency through legally earning and saving money because doing so would do nothing to teach these inmates "their lesson," whatever that means.

Those that are actually attempting to improve society by reforming convicts on the other hand could counter this absurd argument— and possibly disenthrall its adherents— by advocating for a restructuring of just one particular company's method of distributing profits.

Here in North Carolina, a company by the name of Corrections Enterprise is by far the most significant exploiter of inmate labor. This quasi-private company enters into contracts with the North Carolina Department of Public Safety which allows them to employ inmates at a wage rate of less than forty cents per hour to sew uniforms, mix paint, construct road signs, assemble furniture, manufacture eyeglasses, package meat products, make bars of soap, and stamp license plates amongst other things. Their revenue comes from governmental agencies and bureaucrats (i.e. oblivious tax payers) who pay this company for these products that get used by the state, or through the sale of these cheaply made products to other buyers, mostly corporate or institutional purchasers. (Due to low labor costs, Corrections Enterprise is the king of underbidding competitors.) This organization generates impressive annual profits that run very high into the eight figure range. If legislators and administrators are unwilling to tolerate the increase in inmate pay, training, and skill level that could result from allowing other corporations to compete for prisoner labor, another alternative would be to require Corrections Enterprise to designate a significant portion of their profits for the post-secondary education of detainees (or for the replacement of severely antiquated, impractical, and immaterial literature in prison libraries).

Done properly, such measures would appease the socially conservative, right-winged, and frequently irrational few who don't seem to understand that giving convicts a *chance* is not the same as giving them a *handout*. It would placate the classist disciplinarians who intend to perpetuate convicts' status as second-class citizens by keeping both inmates' wages and relative skill levels abysmally low and sometimes non-existent. Such a mandate would also somewhat satisfy detainees, progressive and patriotic philanthropists, and penological activists by giving convicts' the opportunity to transcend and overcome second-class citizenship through intellectual development and collegiate education initiatives.

Additionally, it would pacify the plutocratic legislators who seem to esteem this state's overall fiscal picture over the quality of life of its residents. Both employing inmates and improving the ways in which they're allowed to be compensated, and/or exacting fees from employers of prisoners to fund effective and substantial rehabilitative classes and programs are realistic and executable notions. As my readers may have surmised, the aim of these notions is the disarmament of the opposing forces that are likely to rally against the invocation of my ideas concerning scholastic progression within North Carolina prisons.

Modernizing the Old Model with an Aversion to Bar Lowering

An effective argument has yet to be made in support of what is currently the prison education model's status quo. Most would agree with my claim that this status quo is very dubious, to say the least. It generates a problem that is in desperate need of a solution and it is understandably debatable as to which solution is most likely to be enacted.

Nevertheless, whichever solution is deemed most appropriate should be actualized immediately. Too much time has already been wasted. Too many men have already been denied an education, and as a result of such denial, they've been dangerously criminalized and prisonized. Too many upstanding citizens have been victimized by this process— the manufacturing of undereducated criminals.

This needs to be addressed as soon as possible. This needs to be dealt with expeditiously so that the prison education structure can evolve and more effectively rectify the intellectual and mental deficiencies with which inmates are plagued. Now is the time to act, for the sake of beautifying this state's confined souls, and strengthening the weakest links of the civilizational chain. It's past time for the penal system— which is allegedly centered on the premise of rehabilitation— to adopt more rehabilitative education models. It's past time for the NCDPS/DAC-Prisons to acknowledge and systemically mimic the very few pockets of academic and intellectual progression that are combining the best facet of the old models with more modern ideas, exchanges, and practices to produce identifiable results.

Darrell Allison, president of Parents for Educational Freedom in North Carolina, wrote that the idea behind embracing "the symbiotic relationship that already exists between our traditional and non-traditional [education models] is not to promote one educational model over another, but to show that it takes more than one type of [schooling] to provide a high-quality education to every student." He goes on to state that espousing a mutualistic relationship between theoretical and pragmatic scholastic frameworks will help establish a system in which every student is learning effectively and efficiently. This epitomizes the approach that the NCDPS/DAC-Prison's education program needs to take. Initiating change by simply combining the current education model with progressive practices such as the addition of purposeful and relevant required readings and the introduction of online instruction is a worthy investment with the potential for a vast return.

The advent of online education and required book reports in prison would also serve as a solution to a problem that I've termed *the lowered bar*. As things currently stand, inmates have to expend an absurdly low level of energy in order to obtain a scholastic diploma or certificate. Very little intellectual exercise is required from incarcerated students. The "bar," so-to-speak, is so ubiquitously low that most inmates simply accept that grades depend moreso on attendance than performance. Also, because the vast majority of inmates only want sheepskins, they simply show up to class and bask in the fact that they won't be required to do anything that can reasonably be considered work.

The argument in support of such comparatively low standards is centered on the achievement gap. Proponents of the lowered bar rightfully declare that inmates do not launch toward academic flowering and expansion from the same starting place as their non-incarcerated counterparts. The fact that these inmates are perceived as "behind," and many believe these detainees may have to cover more ground to reach a lower benchmark, supposedly justifies the loosened requirements.

This is actually quite easy to understand. In fact, this posture closely resembles that taken by the state of Florida in 2012. In October of this year, state officials set a goal to have eighty-six percent of white Floridian children at or above grade level in math by 2018, while the goal for black kids was only seventy-four percent. In response to the unrest that resulted from these disparate goals, Sunshine State officials stated that the dissimilar standards reflect the achievement gap.

However, my counter-argument closely resembles that of *Miami Herald* columnist, Leonard Pitts. Mr. Pitts, countering Florida's justification of their racially divergent "bars," wrote "some coaches and athletic directors have noted a steep decline in the number of white kids going out for basketball. They feel as if they cannot compete with their black classmates. What if we addressed that by lowering the rim for white kids? What if we allowed them four points for each made basket? Can you imagine how those white kids would feel whenever they took the court? How long would it be before they internalized the lie that there is something about being white that makes you inherently inferior when it comes to hoops?"

He goes on to write that the problem with this sort of layout, the dilemma behind this sort of order, is it might give individuals the mistaken idea that they carry some ingrained deficiency that renders them unable to operate or compete on the same level as others, even when it's blatantly obvious that this is untrue. He states, "...it burns...to realize people have judged you by a lower standard, especially when you had the ability to meet the higher one all along." This is something with which inmates are quite familiar.

To reward inmates with a diploma, despite intellectual stagnation and *under*exertion, while their non-imprisoned counterparts must undergo at least twelve years of schooling and periodically demonstrate some measure— albeit a very small measure— of intellectual progress in order to earn the same diploma, is menacingly crippling. To lower academic standards in prison to a level below those of an already unimpressive public school system is to subject detainees to a criminality-promoting form of psychological debilitation from which they usually never recover.

The act of lowering the bar serves as a psychotropic mallet. This mallet hammers away at a massively destructive nail, further embedding it into the psyche of these detainees. This nail is made of an inferiority complex, and it is continuously struck until it penetrates deeply into the very core of many prisoners' characters and becomes inseparable from their self-concept. Upon these detainees' release from prison, this mental mallet gains a companion in the form of a huge sledgehammer with unrelenting momentum, a companion that is equally eager to pound the nail of inferiority. This sledgehammer is the unavoidable reality check that makes it clear to the recently released convict that his credentials are absolutely useless.

It's only a matter of time before these individuals are hit with this reality, before they are pummeled by the realization that they've spent years erroneously equating their status as GED certificate recipients with that of Rhodes Scholars. One day they will encounter, and be smashed by, the actual fact that their fake sheepskins are meaningless when separated from intellectual development. They will be candidly informed that their acquisition of these paltry pieces of paper has left them completely unprepared for the free world. This isn't because they were intrinsically inept though. It's because while in prison, an impotent education model led them to believe that these pieces of paper made them superbly capable of tackling adulthood.

Questioning why they were led to believe such a lie will only lead them to one of two solutions: either the world didn't want them to be adequately prepared, or it never believed that they were capable of being adequately prepared. (Both of these solutions solidify the belief that society disfavors them, or is "out to get them," for no apparent reason.) The result of accepting either one of these solutions is the same— fulfillment of harmfully negative expectations. If the prisoners believe they are perceived as incapable, they simply accept it and embrace the falsehood that certain paths in life just aren't for them— one of these paths for which they're now ill-suited happens to be the path of legitimate law-abiding citizenship. If the prisoners believe that it was a concentrated, systematic effort to prevent them from being sufficiently prepared, they become bitter and angry which manifests once again as a rejection of legitimate law-abiding citizenship. Join this with the fact that these ex-convicts are already expected to relapse back into criminal behavior and you have a recipe for creating recidivists.

Instead of trying to enhance the appearance of academic achievement by lowering the bar, the prison education model should concentrate on lifting the students. This task is simplified tremendously, if not completely executed, by making online education available in prison. Schools that live in the cloud do not lower their standards. Students either sink or swim. Such a disposition would force inmates to rise to the occasion; it would give them (give *us*) something to aim for instead of simply praising and glorifying mediocrity and accepting subpar academic executions.

The William and Ida Friday Center for Continuing Education at UNC-Chapel Hill

The William and Ida Friday Center for Continuing Education— referred to henceforth as "The Friday Center"— offers self-paced collegiate correspondence courses to eligible inmates, free of charge, in North Carolina. The correspondence courses are offered through one of eight institutions of the University of North Carolina post-secondary education system; all eight institutions are accredited by the Southern Association of Colleges and Schools. The self-paced courses program is administered by The Friday Center's Credit Programs for Part-time Students Department; Timothy Sanford serves as associate director of this department.

For the most part, The Friday Center's pursuit of higher education for North Carolinian prisoners is honorable and quite commendable. The Center saw an addressable issue and decided to take action in what they believed would be an effective manner. Not only do I admire what I perceive to be their dedication to higher learning, I aim to contribute to the broadening and deepening of their scope and the enhancement of their approach as well as the concentration of their resources. They've given a boatload of inmates the opportunity to be guided through intellectually enhancing scholastic endeavors by qualified instructors, and for this they are well respected and appreciated.

In light of this, there's one flaw, one progress-hindering blemish, within the eligibility requirements of The Friday Center that is worthy of criticism and scrutiny. For reasons unbeknownst to so many, The Friday Center forbids inmates with Class "A" or Class "B" felonies from taking correspondence courses funded through this organization. Inmates classified as such, in pursuit of higher education, must fund their own scholastic endeavors.

On the surface, this seems reasonable, but clarification of this viewpoint's cloudy complexities reveals a fair share of unforeseen complications. Those sentenced under the guise of Class "A" or Class "B" felonies tend to be penalized with substantially lengthy prison sentences— often in excess of ten years. This means that the harmful effects of incarceration will have ample time to take root in the minds and souls of these felons, moreso than anyone else behind prison walls. Enduring such an extensive confinement puts one at a major disadvantage upon his re-entry into society. Serving twenty years in prison leaves one severely handicapped by institutionalization and in more need of academic upliftment than an individual that is released after just three or four years.

A nineteen-year-old child sentenced to a minimum of three years will be released at age twenty-two. Regardless of how much education this teenager receives in prison, he will be young enough, vibrant enough, and undamaged enough to actualize higher education for himself, contribute to his community in a substantive way, and secure a solid career when he leaves prison. A nineteen-year-old sentenced to twenty-two years in prison will be released at age forty-one. At this age, and with his life experiences, he will be gravely impaired by prison life and perniciously uneducated and uncredentialed.

One may be considering the possibility of this inmate finding employment in prison and funding his own education before he's released. This consideration is based on ignorance due to the fact that if he receives incentive wages— minus the price of food and hygiene products— it'll take him close to two and a half years to save up enough money for one credit hour of higher education. Too bad he'll need over one hundred twenty additional credit hours to receive a bachelor's degree. Being forsaken by this system's most momentous and mentally developing, intellectually rehabilitative source— The Friday Center— increases this felon's chances of becoming a recidivist exponentially.

As things currently stand, inmates in situations similar to this latter scenario (inmates such as myself) are denied the opportunity to combat the lasting mental and psychological artillery that incarceration aims at the incarcerated. The inmates that are ineligible for The Friday Center's generous services due to their felony classification are unfortunately situated to spend their post-prison life in a state of second-class citizenship. This assault against upward mobility and societal forgiveness is unnecessary and seemingly insuperable, yet it can easily be corrected by the philanthropic souls that are willing to enact change.

Most of the detainees that I've encountered with pre-prison college credits are coincidentally Class "A" or Class "B" felons. They're not eligible for The Friday Center's services even though they unanimously desire further credit accumulation. They are often obliged to witness eligible detainees disregard, if not disrate, the opportunity given to them by The Friday Center, an opportunity that many ineligible inmates desperately desire. In case you didn't know, the current pool of inmates that are eligible for fully funded correspondence courses shows relatively little interest in post-secondary education.

North Carolinian prisoners with these harsher felony classifications readily sympathize with the May 2011 writings of a Texas prisoner when they meditate on the intellects of those that are eligible for free college courses. This prisoner wrote that "here in Texas, there's a lot of youngsters who have no understanding whatsoever of social relations. Their comprehension level is totally shot...and due to administrative policy, we don't qualify for educational opportunities." Add to this the criminal justice system's tendency to give individuals with higher intelligence levels harsher felony classifications than their less mentally developed counterparts (under the "they-should-have-known-better" umbrella) and one can easily see that The Friday Center's investment in ALL detainees would yield a much better societal return than they're currently generating.

I believe that it would behoove all involved parties if this thoughtful and socially contributive organization didn't become dismissive when ruminating about the intellectual well-being of Class "A" and Class "B" felons

PART THREE

CONCLUSION

> *"A recent poll by the Orlando Parade (March 7, 2010) confirms that more than ninety percent of Americans believe that it is 'important to be personally involved in supporting a cause one believes in' in their communities and in the world at large...Yet those closest to the ground— on the receiving end of this outpouring of generosity— quietly admit that it may be hurting more than helping."*
> -Robert D. Lupton
> *Toxic Charity*

I hold the belief that all fields of study should consist of individuals that are in pursuit of societal and/or global upliftment and progression. From biology and sports medicine to engineering and graphic design, social and intellectual evolution should be the aspiration; a more comfortable, sustainable, and growth-inspiring quality of life should be the goal. This also applies to the field of penology. Studying the origins of lawless tendencies, the ways in which crimes affect civilization, how effective or ineffective a society's method of dealing with crime may be, as well as ways in which to reduce criminality should all be done under the umbrella of human advancement.

Woefully, under such an umbrella, penologists, in tandem with inmate reformists and others that are interested in improving society by refining the tarnished souls that are confined behind prison walls, face many obstacles to these progressive interests. Some of these obstacles are paradigmatic as outlined by Michelle Alexander in *The New Jim Crow: Mass Incarceration in the Age of Colorblindness*; some are financial, as stated in *Prison Profiteers: Who Makes Money From Mass Incarceration*, edited by Tara Herivel and Paul Wright; and some are political as Marc Mauer noted in *Race to Incarcerate*. Although the slipshod and oppressively punitive machine known as the North Carolina penal system is far from being efficient, the fervor of academics, researchers, and activists is nothing less than admirable, if not impressive, in spite of these obstacles.

Sadly, many of these obstacles are beyond the reach of penologists and cannot be combated on a battlefield that is divorced from public opinion, which is where penologists most exercise their influence. Poverty, drug proliferation, extremely biased methods of law enforcement, perceptions of being economically exploited and pigeonholed, low-quality education systems, and overall societal marginalization of "at-risk" individuals are major encumbrances to crime reduction about which penologists alone can do little more than debate and opine. These obstacles must be addressed by society at large. It is the responsibility of this entire nation to aid in the transcendence of these sorts of impediments. All true patriots should heed the call to enrich ALL of their fellow countrymens' quality of life, not just that of a few affluent elites. Unfortunately these responsibilities are neglected and these calls go perpetually unanswered.

Instead of assisting penological experts in their efforts to refine those with criminous dispositions, this society socially and economically assaults people for not capitalizing on opportunities of which they're completely unaware. In response to a question once posed by economist Glenn Loury, I regrettably must say that we ARE willing to cast ourselves as a society that creates criminogenic conditions for some of its members, and then acts out rituals of punishment against them as if engaged in some awful form of human sacrifice. With respect to shaming those that are trapped in these criminogenic conditions, we ARE willing to demonize a population, declare a war against them, and then stand back and heap scorn and disgrace upon them for failing to behave like model citizens while under attack. This must change before progress can be made.

Concerning matters related directly to reformative initiatives enacted within penal institutions, penologists can be quite impactful. Not only are they able to enlighten influential people and initiate paradigm-shifts, but they are also capable of mobilizing their supporters and leading a campaign for inmate reconditioning. Yet, due to either misguided means of data collection, the gathering of extraneous information, yet to be discovered methods of effectively applying the data that has been collected, or unattainable goals, models and theories developed by penologists have had little success in rehabilitating convicts. Prison continues to operate as a system of crime creation and as a garden of lawlessness and immorality. These shortcomings are magnified by the unfavorable stigmas that come along with a criminal conviction— stigmas that motivate people to shine unflattering lights upon those that sincerely seek to educate and morally elevate prisoners.

Policy makers continue to disregard the penal system's ceaseless endorsement of criminality because of such stigmas and unflattering lights. They don't want to be labeled and categorized as one that is excessively "soft" on crime, even though their present predilection (not rehabilitating inmates, refraining from educating and empowering at-risk individuals, blocking efforts to intellectually ripen and ethically enhance the downtrodden, etc.) epitomizes the "gentle" approach. These legislators make a show of being rigidly anti-crime by vouching for mass incarceration and assailing individual criminals. They don't seem to realize that their practice of incarcerating and vilifying those labeled as "criminals" only fuels crime; demonizing the individual only strengthens the act. They are, by definition, soft on crime because they focus solely on individuals painted in criminous colors while refusing to attack crime itself with full force.

However, this habit of obviously promoting what they claim to be fighting against isn't limited to domestic illegality. This habit serves as the foundation for America's newly defined modern warfare. Many individuals firmly believe that their definition of "war" is accurate and reliable. Most people here in the United States characterize war as something that's between a mere struggle or competition between adverse forces, and open and declared, definitely hostile and probably armed conflict between groups, states, or regimes. Even though people have different experiences pertaining to war– from simply seeing romantic war scenes acted out on television to actually partaking in gun battles while enlisted in the military– few individuals in our great civilization refute the idea that war basically involves one "side" fighting in some fashion against another "side" using weaponry that is contextually fitting and appropriate. Although this basic definition holds true for the most part, the way in which America *identifies* warring factions has changed dramatically in recent years.

Up until the 1960s, when America was thought to be at war, our enemies were typically defined using geographical descriptions. This means that incidents categorized as national warfare occurred between America and this place or that place, between the United States and people born in this or that location, or between the inhabitants of our particular portion of Earth's surface and the rulers of a different portion of Earth's surface. Even soldiers fighting in the Civil War were generally differentiated by their birthplaces and residences– troops were born and raised in one part of the country while their opposing countrymen/combatants were reared in another.

This tendency to identify combative parties according to their location changed in the 1960s when a new type of American warfare was introduced. This decade gave birth to a new means of identifying warring camps. For the first time in history, under the presidency of Lyndon B. Johnson, the United States officially declared war on an abstraction and directed offensive war initiatives towards something other than a flesh and blood adversary. In this war there was no country on which we could drop bombs to guarantee our success, nor was our foe identified according to its domicile or its nationality. In the 1960s President Johnson implemented the War on Poverty and unknowingly restructured the way in which national enemies are identified, a restructuring that has had devastating consequences.

By avowing this war on an invisible enemy (poverty, like the wind, is invisible; only its effects are discernible), by blazoning this war on an assailant that possesses substance apart from an object, the framework was set for future wars such as the War on Drugs, the War on Terror, and the War on Crime. Fighting concepts, ideas, and faceless enemies such as poverty has had, and is having, a direct and meaningful impact on the lives of American civilians.

With poverty being such a formless and abstruse antagonist, conservative ideologues responded to President Johnson's declaration of war by resorting to tactics of old. Being accustomed to defining national enemies according to ancestry and geography, they *created* an identifiable face for this abstraction and defined its birthplace, heritage, and current location. Anyone born in this place or residing in this location with this heritage was in turn labeled as the personification of poverty and therefore demonized and treated like an enemy combatant. (Of course, on the heels of the Civil Rights Movement this "place," this identity-producing location, was determined to be any and basically every impoverished and mostly chocolate community.) By labeling and demonizing poor people under the "poverty-personified-arch," the ideologues were able to steer and coordinate the war.

For example, the 1964 War on Poverty bill included provisions for Job Corps, a program that was supposed to provide education and job-training for poor people. However, the conservative establishment at the time only herded poor and working poor delinquents and miscreants towards this program. They ensured that Job Corps consisted of young destitute people that had already confirmed they were averse to instruction and training. As a result, Job Corps essentially became a co-educational prison while politically right-winged zealots assigned blame for this programs failure to the poor youths themselves. The chorus of "I told you so" coming from conservatives was deafening, along with their assertions that the socioeconomically underprivileged

171

Job Corps "students" (i.e. detainees) were incompetent, lazy and incapable of transcending their lots. This caused further demonization and institutionalization of poor youths which made them even poorer, spreading impoverishment and therefore solidifying their position as enemies in America's War on Poverty. In other words, poverty was in effect promoted when conservatives transformed the War on Poverty into a War on Certain Identifiable Poor People.

The same tactics used to actualize this transformation in the 1960s were deployed during President Ronald Reagan's War on Drugs in the 1980s. Like Johnson, Reagan failed to identify effectively what his war on this abstraction truly meant. His actions didn't clarify whether he aimed to combat the importation of drugs, to address and eliminate people's desire to use drugs, to acknowledge and rectify the circumstances that make drug-dealing a viable option for many Americans, nor whether he wished to expand access to drug counselors and clinics. This lack of clarity set the stage for another antagonistic abstraction to be identified and assigned a face. Already viewed negatively by social and political bigots, it was decided that this "face" would be that of the black American male. And because the origins of this face were once again determined to be impoverished and predominantly minority communities, racially biased social conservatives amped up police presence in these neighborhoods despite the fact that drug use and distribution was (and is) more prominent and populous in white suburbia.

In addition to a heightened police presence, legislators passed laws that intensified the penalties for drugs associated with these communities while punition for the more "vanilla" drugs remained relatively lenient. As many may know, this increased and asymmetrical enforcement of lopsided and excessively punitive drug laws led to more arrests in these neighborhoods. This, in turn, led to lower property values and thereupon decreased public school funding and caused the upcoming generation in these neighborhoods to be even less educated and less employable and more likely to resort to illegal drug use and distribution. Once again the conservative establishment, because of its covert biases, fertilized the very enemy on which war had been declared. Their inability to effectively fight a harmful yet abstract idea only heightened crime and transformed the War on Drugs into a War on Tangible Communities That Have Been Victimized by Drugs. (Incarcerated Thinkers have argued that the War on Drugs was much more depredating than the War on Poverty due to Ronald Reagan's undeniable allegiance to the socially conservative paradigm.)

The practice of defining America's opponents in battle, of personifying and objectifying an abstraction on which America has declared war, has not lessened in intensity as time has progressed. Au contraire, the twenty-first century began with the most fascinating example of this practice to date: the War on Terror.

The first step taken in this war was to incarnate terror itself. This was accomplished by defining the former leader of Iraq— Saddam Hussein— as a terrorist and public enemy number one in our anti-terror crusade. Military leaders, under the authority of former president George W. Bush, then determined that using terror itself as an offensive strategy would ensure our victory over this enemy. In fighting Iraqi people, that were angered by the Western tendency to police the world, these leaders decided *more* policing would solve the problems caused by such anger. In partaking in combat with people who were anti-American because of America's incessant desire to impose its will, our government concluded that further "will imposition" was the key.

High ranking officials here in the United States spoon-fed the American people the belief that our enemies would refrain from attacking us in our homeland if we took the initiative to attack them first in their homeland even though all evidence confirmed that such preventative attacks and invasions would only lead

173

to more terrorism. As a result of such idiotic reasoning, from 2003 to 2009 American troops slaughtered 0.5 percent of Iraq's non-combatant civilian population alone. Percentagewise, this is equivalent to murdering every single citizen living in St. Louis, New Orleans, Orlando, Tampa, and Newark.

However, these convoluted tactics, as well as the War on Terror itself, outlived the elimination of Saddam Hussein's dictatorship. In post-Iraq-war United States, the definition of terrorism is still being assigned a face; it has expanded to include almost one billion people. Mostly due to the ways in which the prolonged activities of individuals such as Osama bin Laden has been illustrated and reported, terrorism now encompasses almost all Muslims in the eyes of mainstream America. For confirmation, consider that a young kid with an Islamic name (Muhammad) had his plan to detonate a shoe-bomb thwarted by law enforcement officials while major media outlets undeniably labeled him as a terrorist, even though nobody was injured. But a white, non-Muslim male from New England brutally murdered almost two dozen children in an elementary school in Connecticut and these same media sources expended extra effort to inform the public that this particular school shooting was NOT a terrorist attack. The obvious implication is that only Islamic individuals can be terrorists, despite how terroristic the actions of a non-Muslim may be.

Here in North Carolina, and under the guise of "religious freedom," Republican legislators recently attempted to implement a law establishing this state's official religion as Christianity (House Joint Resolution 494). This implementation was in response to criticism aimed at Republicans who sought to open congressional meetings with a Christian prayer. When asked if she would support a Muslim offering a prayer before the state legislature, conservative state representative Michele Presnell responded with "No, I do not condone terrorism...[we] need to start taking a stand on our religious freedom or it will be whisked away from us."

How counterproductive is it to encourage religious freedom by introducing laws that limit religious freedom? How counterproductive is it to combat terrorism by using insinuation to add one billion Muslims to the list of known terrorists? Too many ideologically influential Americans seem to ignore the fact that demonizing Islam in such a way has given Muslims and non-Muslims alike further incentive to dislike America; it supports the agenda of violent radicals and it energizes terrorism.

The effects of the actions taken against "terror" are not aligned with the United States' stated position in our war against this abstraction, but they're perfectly aligned with the effects of past actions taken against what now seem to be out-of-style abstractions. This nation's decision-makers and representatives are invigorating terror in the same way that their predecessors enlivened poverty and drug proliferation. (Just to be fair here, I must note that while conservatives were making these tactical and oppressive moves, the soft and sensitive liberals were busy being soft and sensitive.) My fellow statesmen should not make the same mistakes when approaching the abstract, yet less glamorous, domestic conflict known as the War on Crime.

Currently, legislators and administrators here in the state of North Carolina mainly avoid enacting reformative measures. They fear the inevitable political backlash that would erupt from both the voting blocs and the thousands of individuals employed by the criminal justice system at various levels who appreciate their current job security, which is likely to erode in the face of diminished criminality and recidivism reduction. Such avoidance is the first step in personifying crime. This must be recognized and opposed. They should not be allowed to humanize lawlessness by turning the War on Crime into a War on Past and Present Convicts. Local decision-makers should seek to learn from history instead of repeating it; they should avoid undergirding crime and use this book's content to debride the toxic growth that is North Carolina's treatment of both convicted criminals and crime itself.

No longer should this state's lawmakers rely entirely on traditional penologists to help shape criminal justice policies. These orthodox penologists rely solely on mass incarceration advocates to compile data for research related purposes, lean heavily on lawmen to provide information on the effects of arrest and detention, and depend exclusively on lawyers and judges to paint a picture of courtroom mechanisms. Contemporary penologists, convict criminologists, and Incarcerated Thinkers are inclined to gather multifaceted data from diverse sources and produce ideas and suggest trajectories that are verifiably better for society than the current state of criminal justice affairs. They stick to this inclination regardless of how well such ideas and trajectories will be viewed and received.

These intellectuals are able to remain steadfast and at the forefront of modernity for multiple reasons. First, they are academics, not politicians; they aren't plagued by the same anti-progressive hindrances that afflict policy-makers. Also, their intellectual profession isn't guided by public opinion. They are uniquely poised to operate independently, only being marginally, if at all, affected by public consensus. This means that they value the art of pleasing people less than the science of pursuing evolution– at least as far as their cerebral vocation is concerned.

Finally, contemporary penologists, convict criminologists, and Incarcerated Thinkers have transcended the cronyism that is diffused throughout the criminal justice system. They are capable of functioning without the nepotistic influences that exist amongst police officers, district and prosecutorial attorneys, defense attorneys (especially public defenders), judges, and prison officials. These three related specialists are encouraged to traverse whichever path their intellectual activity leads them down, regardless of whether or not they'll be "accepted" by their cohorts. Their relatively free reign makes them well-positioned to herd the philanthropic cavalry towards prisoner rehabilitation, to lead the humanitarian trailblazers to universal inmate reform mainly by soliciting and weighing the authentic, organic and articulate inputs of informed critical thinkers.

The only obstructions are those that are self-induced. Up until this point, few beyond a handful of activists and imprisoned freedom fighters have been dedicated to making such considerations. This too must change. Legislative and academic elites must begin to use ALL of the resources to which they have access, especially when their decisions directly dictate the direction of institutions that are structured on and around human lives.

Notwithstanding, I applaud those scholars whose actions already reflect an extensive use of non-traditional resources, especially pertaining to gloomy fields of study such as criminal justice and prison advocacy (scholars such as Saundra D. Westervelt of UNC-Greensboro and Kimberly J. Cook of UNC-Wilmington). I commend the penologists and criminologists that actively study penal systems with the hope of reducing recidivism through inmate reform. This is a very unpopular and controversial undertaking, but these intelligent minds and spirits do not allow themselves to be dissuaded. This is because they are true philanthropic and patriotic academics that sincerely believe in societal advancement and see prisoner rehabilitation as a means of actualizing it. However, as I've outlined, there are improvements that need to be made concerning penological practices, academia's flexibility, and societal perceptions. Penologists should once again gravitate towards studying criminals and discovering and pursuing the elimination of the causes of criminality as the "positive school" of criminology attempted to do during the late nineteenth century.

It's important that the convicts who desire and are capable of reform, those that have consciously worked to become what Antonio Gramsci defined as "organic intellectuals," contribute to this school of

177

thought. These contributions, at the very least, should consist of informing penologists of the collateral damage that comes with their outpouring of misguided and misinformed humanitarianism, damage that has been unaddressed for far too long now. It's time for people like myself to start shouting the politically incorrect truth which is that most inmates are helpless, unreachable, and averse to rehabilitation, and inmate reformists should focus their energy on the currently disregarded "collateral damage"— the inmates that do not fall into this category of ineptitude. Above-average inmates are who rehabilitative measures should be, but currently are not, designed around. This design flaw sums up the reason why prison continuously fails to positively recondition its inhabitants.

It is my hope that my readers are not trapped into thinking that the few inmates that can be reached, that embrace beneficial reconditioning and are most likely to avoid recidivism once released, are testaments of prison's rehabilitative nature. Do not allow these exceptions to underpin false notions pertaining to inmate reform, notions that have been thoroughly disproven. The current criminality-inspiring aspect of the penal system is neither discredited nor undermined by the rare instances of inmate exceptionalism. To the contrary, it depends on it. (Consider that a recidivism rate of 100% would shine too harsh of a light on the people who benefit from mass incarceration and current penal system structures.)

These exceptions could potentially become the rule if traditional mainstream penologists placed more value on the input and outlooks of convict criminologists and above-average detainees, and if more people willingly assisted contemporary penologists in their efforts to improve society through inmate habilitation. For this end, this book has been made available to penal researchers with the hope that it will be used in our War Against Crime. This text is an attack on harmful civic illegality. It is a warning against North Carolina's current practice of boosting criminality by ensuring the existence of second class citizenship through inmate oppression.

This work is also a scattershot lesson that should expand the language that is used to examine, describe and propel the education of the imprisoned. The ideas presented here should create and supercharge platforms that cultivate critical cerebral exercise amongst the incarcerated. They should also fortify prison's currently weak version of what Harvard education professor Richard Elmore calls the "instructional core"— the skills of the teacher, the engagement of the students, and the rigor of the curriculum. To succeed at such tasks, prosecutors must become ministers of justice, not just administers of convictions; teachers must become engaged public intellectuals, not just educated bystanders; legislators must become nutritious fertilizers, not just societal excrement; and prisoners must become thoughtfully critical organic catalysts, not just test-takers.

I'm currently positioned in a way that allows me to clearly observe this system's faulty instructional core, to see through the bafflingly attractive delusory coat that drapes the shoulders of the North Carolina Department of Public Safety/Division of Adult Correction-Prisons' scholastic, leisure, and rehabilitative programs. Unfortunately, the only people that ever gaze from this vantage point are poor decision-makers or those that have made regrettable mistakes, and as a consequence they (we) have been societally demonized and stripped of their (our) democratic voices and gregarious standings. Nonetheless, the voices of those that are seemingly obsessed with alleviating unnecessary social misery, suppression, and institutionalization cannot, and will not, be silenced regardless of where they (we) scream from or the stifling filters through which they're (we're) forced to communicate.

We will aid in the evolution of the penal system, subscribe to the eradication of public and private misdeeds, and augment the position of those that support the instatement and retroactive application of a strict and efficient parole system. Additionally, we, as Incarcerated Thinkers, will complement the argument against those North Carolinians currently seeking to repeal the Racial Justice Act, and disconfirm certain state senators' (such as E.S. Newton's and Shirley B. Randleman's) stated motives for pursuing the further disenfranchisement of ex-convicts. Ours is a quest to champion the empowerment of the underclass, to contribute to the strengthening of those labeled as this state's weakest links. Please know that this strengthening is contingent upon the removal of the glass ceiling that currently hovers over the practical intellectual revolution that's brewing in the hearts and minds of the downtrodden. I implore all to ignore the mendacity of the status-quo preservers and explore the benefits of uplifting and educating the most capable members of North Carolina's most maltreated subculture.

It is my goal to contribute to this much needed sociological subdivision known as penology by assisting the experts, by making myself available, by giving my input. But in order for this to be accomplished, in order for my progressive goals to be reached, in the words of R.D. Lupton, it's vital that students and experts within this field of study recognize that "the poor, no matter how destitute, have enormous untapped capacity," and that penologists "find it, be inspired by it, and build upon it."

AFTERWORD

A LETTER TO MY NEPHEW

Joe Jr,

      I don't know the color in which your memory will paint my presence in your life as your mother's incarcerated brother, nor can I predict how far along on Life's journey you will have progressed by the time that my words are made clear to you. I'm not sure if these words of mine will have a significant impact upon your existential paradigm, and I'm unaware of which path(s) this paradigm of yours will compel you to traverse. Whether you will embrace the life of the streets or the Life of the Mind, if you'll grow to admire George W. Bush or Huey P. Newton, or whether you will frequent Silicon Valley or the Vegas strip are all unknown as of these writings.

      However, I am very aware of my desire to contribute to your overall well-being by informing you of my interpretation of, and experiences with, society's hidden yet well-nourished demon: urban criminality and our nation's method of dealing with it. I want you to avoid this demon entirely. I want you to remain in touch with your ever-evolving dreams Joe, with the deepest fibers of your mind's aspirations, and not allow the world to force you to become someone that's incapable of understanding what I mean by this. I don't want controllable circumstances to turn you cold and mean, to kill that thing that makes you laugh the laugh of the joyful, the laugh of the fulfilled, and the laugh of the intellectually successful.

      Anything that hinders this should be fought against. I do not want you to cerebrally pigeon-hole yourself at society's coercion, to bury yourself in a grave of criminous self-genocide simply because your environment provides you with the shovels. It is my hope that you don't define yourself extrinsically, that you don't measure your self-worth using a ruler notched with self-deprecating superficialities. Doing so may result in transcendental anger, a state of nondemonstrable rage that you will either turn inward or project outward, the aftermath being a diminishment of soulful beauty on a variety of levels. Understand that your plight as a black male in this age, as the grandson of baby-boomers in this contemporary world, will be both complex and unique– try looking at the older generations for the antique version of this plight.

The major domestic powers of a previous time hatefully categorized your grandfather, my father, as a "nigger" throughout his childhood. Because of such categorization he wasn't qualified for bank loans, he was distrusted and despised by the majority, tagged as unfit to attend prestigious universities, denied government assistance, and targeted by law enforcement officials with bad intentions. Being labeled in this way is why your mother's father was considered incapable of any work beyond manual labor for paltry wages, regarded as unequipped for lucrative and non-physical employment, deemed ineligible to vote, deserving of economic exploitation, and unfairly saddled with debt. Being identified as a "nigger" is why your grandfather was viewed as a hairy and grotesque wart on the otherwise pretty face of this nation. An aversion to whites and a little luck are the only reasons why he wasn't shot, stabbed, dismembered, or lynched.

This vicious American legacy, this very American tradition of classifying blacks as savages, as malicious and wicked brutes, as "niggers," has transformed. You, unlike your grandfather, are unlikely to be told that you can't enter an establishment or drink from a water fountain or get sexually involved with a white woman only because your skin is too dark. The metamorphosis that this heritage of "non-WASP-debasement" has undergone is the reason why you probably will never encounter a Bull O'Conner with a fire hose or a Californian governor such as Ronald Reagan voting against civil rights initiatives or a George Wallace blocking your entrance into a university or a Strom Thurman dressed in Ku Klux Klan apparel.

Nevertheless, you as a black male, as a mere condition of your existence, run the risk of being eaten by the monster that blatant racial oppression and brutality has morphed into, a leviathan that goes by the names of *criminal justice* and *mass incarceration*. Being marked as a criminal will allow banks, schools, and municipalities to reject you. It allows employers to ignore you, the majority to distrust, dehumanize, and despise you, and the police to violate you. Such a designation legitimizes discrimination, causing you to suffer the modern day version of the societal atrocities to which your grandfather was exposed as a young man.

"Criminal" is the new "nigger" and the socially conservative Establishment is quite eager to perpetuate this reality at the expense of your welfare. There are people in this country that will prosper off of your personal calamities if you allow them to do so Joe. There are people that will benefit from the hell that you will be forced to endure if you believe that Lil Wayne is "real," that 50 Cent's songs and his public persona are something more than sources of entertainment, or that pistols or drug money may augment your character. Adopting this belief system, one rooted in criminality, is akin to designating yourself as prey to tough-on-crime legislation such as "three strikes," "truth in sentencing," and "mandatory minimum" sentencing laws– all tremendously sharp teeth in the mouth of the Old Guard.

For example, consider Corrections Corporation of America (CCA) — a private, for-profit prison corporation. They make money by building and operating prisons inhabited by "criminals." In order for them to get paid by taxpayers someone has to be locked up; the more people that get incarcerated, the better that their bottom line looks. Up until recently, CCA was a member of the American Legislative Exchange Council (ALEC). ALEC is a public-private legislative partnership whose membership is overwhelmingly comprised of conservative Republican state lawmakers, over 300 of the nation's largest corporations and influential law/lobbying firms. This organization was behind the "No More Sanctuary Cities for Illegal Immigrants Act," the "Voter I.D. Act" (see the 2012 presidential campaign), and the "Stand Your Ground Act" (see Trayvon Martin). When ALEC's

184

proposals, which include but aren't limited to the aforementioned "teeth," succeeded in increasing the prison population, guess who made money....Corrections Corporation of America.

These organizations— their members, employees, and investors— want to see you in prison Joe. They stand to be empowered by your incarceration. They want you to break the law, to commit crimes, to join an urban street gang, to believe the nonsense that most rappers are spewing so that their bank accounts as well as their influence can keep growing. With you in prison these conservative ideologues can feel morally superior and say that they are better and more important than you are. Don't allow them to "Jim Crow" you. Don't let yourself become anyone's twenty-first century "nigger." Rebel at the idea that you can't be a part of other groups, non-criminous groups, and balk at any assertion that implies that you will never reach self-actualization.

Create yourself at your own volition. Construct your identity through discretionary action. Be who you choose to be, regardless of what or who society or your culture seems to be choosing for you. Luxuriate in whatever you might be calling yourself at any particular time, but in the words of Henry Gates Jr., "do so in order to come out the other side, to experience a humanity" that is neither faceless nor reducible to exterior facades.

If you ever find yourself becoming what this letter is warning you against, embrace open-mindedness and mental progression above all. Allow yourself to be a facilitator of change in the same way that Ricky "Freeway" Ross initiated the awakening of the champion of prison education and literary programs, Ms. Jac Brown, founder of "Jac Brown's House of Books." Be fueled and motivated by inactive critics, judgmental finger-pointers, and imperialistic autocrats. Reject nonsense, increase self-knowledge, and pursue self-enrichment. When you're old enough to fully comprehend a thorough explanation of why I've been absent from your life for so long, I hope that it brings you even a small measure of understanding, at long last, of why I see the world with such mordant lucidity, and of why I believe that it's vital for you to be flexible enough to do the same when the need to do so arises.

Upon my exodus from this emotionally torturous and mentally arid penal system, I plan to assist you and your sisters, my nieces, Brianna and Jakayla; I hope to aid in the personal development that I'm sure the three of you are capable of realizing. Until such a time arrives, know that you are greatly esteemed.

—Uncle Ty
Johnson Correctional Institution
January 1, 2013
Month 77

ACKNOWLEDGEMENTS

Praise and Honor to my intellectual heroes
of past and present:
Harry Belafonte', William Barber, Steve Jobs, Mark
Zuckerberg, Richard Branson, Angela Davis, Maya
Angelou, Cornel West, Henry Louis Gates Jr., Michelle
Alexander, Christopher Hitchens, Warren Buffett, Andrea
Dworkin, Alexis de Tocqueville, Friedrich Nietzsche,
Martin Luther King Jr., Malcolm X, Barack and Michelle
Obama, bell hooks, Elijah Anderson, Hugh Heffner,
Michael Eric Dyson, Nelson Mandela and the beautifully
gifted Asia Carrera.

Most importantly, much love to:
Mrs. Linda Mae Carlson, Ms. S. Campbell, Ms. Carol,
Ms. Miln, Ms. Anne Faul, C. Leaming, D.B. Coffin, my
goofy sister with the infectious laugh, Sabrina; my
supportive and beloved mother, Ann G. Baker; and my
wise, caring and highly respected father, E.J.;
from fingertip to fingertip and all in between!

I would like to thank these former and current inmates who truly contributed to my personal growth: Ronald "Junior" Bland, Kevin "Bruh" Shaw, John "Doc" Dye, James "The Fraze" Frazier, and fellow essayist, contributor and Incarcerated Thinker, J. Vincent Hurley.

My writings are the fruit of our many intellectual exchanges. I'm forever grateful that Fate allowed our paths to cross; this work is for you all as well as the other painfully silent screams of society's countless, forgotten souls.

To Terrence Foster, Roodchill Pierre, Thea Newman, and concerning all of my brothers and sisters still locking down for count, walking to chow, getting unwarranted write-ups, wearing Bob Barker shower shoes, waiting for mail call....Know that hard work produces valuable fruit.

Finally, I would like to apologize to the people that convicts have victimized, to the families that we've torn apart and for the painful tears that we've caused. Most of us are truly sorry, even those of us that just don't know how to show it.

ABOUT THE AUTHORS

—T. Lamont Baker is currently serving a minimum of 271 months. He was incarcerated on August 17, 2006, at the age of nineteen. At the time of these writings, Mr. Baker had yet to locate an attorney that was willing to aid him in his pursuit of a sentence commutation. As things currently stand he isn't scheduled to be released until March 24, 2029. He is an autodidact whose scholastic credentials include a high school diploma from Riverside High School in Durham, North Carolina, and a variety of career diplomas accumulated since he's been imprisoned. He openly welcomes all criticisms and critiques, and he encourages all of his readers to correspond with him at their hearts' desire. He has pledged to respond to all letters as time permits.

—Essayist J. Vincent Hurley has an associate's degree in General Education from Fayetteville Technical Community College, and a bachelor's degree in Applied Science/Recreation and Leisure Studies from Mount Olive College. He has been incarcerated since 2007. The earliest date on which he will be eligible for release is in the summer of 2026. He welcomes all correspondence.

As of these writings, inmates T. Lamont Baker #0915700 and J. Vincent Hurley #1097591 both were housed at Johnston Correctional Institution, 2465 US Hwy 70 West, Smithfield, NC 27577. For a current mailing address search these inmates (using their name and identification number) on the following website: www.doc.state.nc.us/offenders/

"The vilest deeds like poison weeds
Bloom well in prison air;
It is only what is good in man
That wastes and withers there."

—*Oscar Wilde*
"The Ballad of Reading Gaol"

SUGGESTED READINGS BY CURRENT OR PAST PRISON INMATES:

Makes Me Wanna Holla: A Young Black Man In America
By: Nathan McCall

Looking For A Way Out
By: Michael Norwood aka Minkah A. Abubakar

Why So Many Black Men Are In Prison
By: Demico Booth

A Question Of Freedom
By: R. Dwayne Betts

Soledad Brother: The Prison Letters Of George Jackson
By: George Jackson

13916284R00117

Made in the USA
San Bernardino, CA
10 August 2014